Spend Smart

Bill Keenan
billk@finhealthrx.com

ISBN # 0-9713073-1-9

Published by: Premier Institute for Financial Freedom, Inc.
1061 Main Street
North Huntingdon, PA 15642
724-861-5468

TABLE OF CONTENTS

> # CHAPTER ONE
> ## INTRODUCTION

Financial freedom - it means different things to different people, but most of us have similar financial objectives. We strive for the typical American Dream - have a nice home, send the kids to college, save for retirement. A comfortable retirement is the ultimate goal for most Americans. Unfortunately, most Americans are failing to achieve this goal.

Why is this happening? There are many related causes but financial failure ultimately boils down to one simple fact. **People fail financially because they fail to save and invest for the future!**

Now there are numerous financial "self-help" books. Most of these books, however, mistakenly assume the reason people fail financially is because they don't know how to invest. While such books are certainly good intentioned, the authors of Spend Smart feel that investment advice is useless for most people. Why? **People do not fail financially simply because they don't know how to intelligently invest money - the journey to financial failure begins because people do not know how to intelligently SPEND MONEY!**

Welcome to Spend Smart™! The purpose of this book is to help people achieve financial independence. To become financially independent, you must invest money. Investing however, is not the focus of this book. Why? Simply put, most people spend as much or more than they make each month. Most Americans have no money left over each month to invest. **If you have no money to invest, how will investment advice help you?**

Spend Smart instead focuses on the area of your life where you have the greatest opportunity to **impact your financial situation immediately!** This area is of course, spending. Applying the strategies in this book will allow you to reduce your spending without diminishing your lifestyle. In other words, you can still do and have the things you want and need - - you'll simply spend less. By Spending Smart, you can liberate money you were previously spending. This money can then be used for investment or for any other financial goals you have.

As part of the introduction, it is important to understand a simple concept. No single Spend Smart strategy or one-time use of a strategy will change your financial future by itself. Some of the strategies will seem insignificant to you. I mean, if you can save $33 a year by turning your oven off ½ hour prior to the end of cooking time is this really going to propel you to financial freedom? Some of the strategies will seem silly. Isn't the idea of turning the water off when you brush your teeth (saving the average family $75 per year) getting a little carried away?

Spend Smart is about choices. You decide what your goals are. You decide what strategies you can employ with a minimum amount of effort. We are confident however, that most people can painlessly reduce their current spending from 10 to 40 percent by applying a consistent variety of strategies.

Think of your wallet or pocketbook as a bucket. Every month your employer pours money into it. You pour money out of it into different areas - food, clothing, cars, insurance, utilities, etc. Your money is leaking out, and most of us don't even notice specific holes because the holes are so tiny. Unfortunately, your money bucket has many holes in it. Now, if you could plug two or three holes, it wouldn't make much difference. The objective of Spend Smart is to help you plug as many holes as possible, every month, so you can keep more of your money.

Does this sound good to you? This is the promise of Spend Smart. Now we're going to test you, to see if you really are motivated enough about changing your financial future that you will change your spending. Motivation is important because in order to be successful with Spend Smart, you must be motivated to want more than a quick fix or one-time approach.

The good news is that anyone, regardless of income or expenses, can significantly improve their financial picture. In fact, I believe that many people who follow Spend Smart and consistently apply it in their lives can become millionaires! The bad news is there is no "Silver Bullet". There is no single idea that will change your life immediately. It takes a lot of ideas used over a long period of time.

Here's the "test" of your motivation. Take a quick look at some Spend Smart strategies. They illustrate that the concept that consistent use of a strategy over time can begin building meaningful financial results.
10 plus one ways that almost everyone can save at least $100 this year

1) Purchase 10 articles of clothing at thrift shops or garage sales instead of paying department store prices.

2) Join your electric company's energy-saver program.

3) Brown-bag your lunch 2 times a month.

4) Replace two gallons of milk each week with powdered milk.

5) Join SHARE of FARE For All Volunteer / Food Co-op program.

6) Learn to change your own oil in both cars.

7) Use half the manufacturers recommended amount of laundry detergent, dishwasher soap, toothpaste, and shampoo.

8) Unplug the refrigerator in the garage or basement where you are keeping drinks, etc. cold.

9) Get a freezer so you can buy in bulk.

10) Eliminate hot/warm water washing.

11) Replace name brand cereal with store brand cereal.

Are you still with us? If you think things like "couponing" are too trivial for your time and are ready to toss this book aside, first ask yourself one question:

Do You Have a Plan for Achieving Financial Independence? Is it Working? Are you Making Enough Money to Succeed with it?

96% of people who follow traditional financial ideas are failing financially. Only 4% of Americans at age 65 make more than $35,000. Now where do you want to be at age 65? DO your dreams call for more than $35,000 per year in income? Or can you exist happily on $12,000 per year (median annual senior citizen income).

If you don't currently have a plan that will make you one of the 4% who succeed financially, shouldn't you at least consider an alternative? Spend Smart is different than any financial self-help book you have ever read. We have a step-by-step process you can follow to achieve financial independence, regardless of your income.

First we will walk you through a goal-setting process so you are clear on where you want to end up. Then we will teach you Spend Smart Strategies. You will pick the ones that make sense to you. Next you will learn how to effectively do the things that make millionaires successful. Finally, we will teach you how to turn Spend Smart Strategies into cold cash in your hand, each and every month.

Some of these strategies listed above will seem reasonable for you to apply and some won't. Either way is fine. If you chose to follow these eleven strategies however, or ones like them, you'll have an extra $1200 in your pocket each year. When you learn the true Value of a Dollar, you'll see that these eleven strategies are actually worth as much as if you got a $1692 raise!

Now these are "small" strategies. They don't individually amount to large amounts of money. Some strategies such as strategies revolving around buying cars, insurance and debt can be worth hundreds or thousands of dollars themselves. The power of Spend Smart is the power of MASSIVE ACTION – the power of numbers.

Recognize however that it is exactly these types of "small" Spend Smart strategies that tens of thousands of people across the country are using to achieve financial results that many would believe to be impossible. Impressive success stories abound. Financial success via Spend Smart is also driven by attitudes.

Your Attitude has a Huge Impact on your Spend Smart Success

Spend Smart Attitudes include the following:

<u>Ten Ideas for Spend Smart Living</u>

1. Roll up your sleeves - working towards a thrifty lifestyle and maintaining success takes consistent effort and hard work. The alternative of convenience is tempting but expensive - don't put off until tomorrow for tomorrow never comes - say hello to tomorrow today!

2. Organize your world - list-making is the key - list items to buy and stick to the list - organizing closets, refrigerators, shelves, etc. keeps you aware of what you have. Buying things you don't need is one of the greatest robbers of wealth.

3. Use what you have first! Look under your kitchen sink – you probably have enough cleaning supplies to clean for a year without buying anything. If we want to save money why waste money on things that will just take up space? Think of the stuff that's in various kitchen, bathroom and bedroom drawers - do you randomly walk around and stick dollar bills in drawers? Of course not - use things up - you will have fun in the process!

4. Waste not! If you don't need something, find someone who does, give it to Goodwill. Better yet, sell it to one of the many fine second-hand store chains that are popping up around the country.

5. Be creative, especially in cooking. Don't be afraid to experiment.

6. Learn Prices (Use our Price Alert Scorecard) - helps you keep perspective when you think you've spotted a "good deal". Watch the

register as your items are rung up - most scanner errors are in the favor of the retailer - Why - because items are on sale less often then they are at regular price.

7. Presentation is everything - do things different to improve their appearance be it food, furniture or clothes. It helps you feel like you are getting more for your money.

8. Attitude Adjustment - Have fun doing this - everything you do to be thrifty, every dollar you save, gets you closer to the goal of financial independence than you would have been. Learn why each dollar you save is the most valuable dollar you'll ever have.

9. Fight Impulse - adopt the opposite of the Nike motto - "Just DON'T Do It". When the urge to make an impulse purchase strikes, don't be afraid to walk away.

10. Don't be surprised if and when you "fall off the wagon".

This book is the result of hundreds of hours of research. The author also "walks the talk". I can tell you from personal experience and the stories of many Spend Smart students…

SPEND SMART WORKS!

Stick with us for a few hours. Open your mind to the possibilities of Spend Smart. Once you finish this book, then you can make a good judgement about whether the Spend Smart way will help you succeed.

We want to encourage the reader to begin their own continuing research on saving money on spending. What you learn in Spend Smart can change your financial future. If you use this as a foundation for further learning, your success will be multiplied.

You will become the best expert on how to Spend Smart given your specific circumstances. If you can figure out how to keep more of the money you bring home each month, you have the power to control your financial destiny. We wish you all the best as you embark on this exciting journey!

CHAPTER TWO
Why Spend Smart?

Our hope with Spend Smart is to help you start on a journey. If you choose the right path for this journey, it can lead you to financial freedom. This path starts of course with learning the Spend Smart way.

Before we begin this journey, it is important to understand why. Why should you Spend Smart? What is the objective, what is the goal? If we don't have a strong reason for doing something, then commitment will be lacking. Without commitment, success will not be achieved. Just as when you begin a trip in your car…before you figure out your path, your route, you first look at where you want to go…what your goal is.

As part of this process, you need to define your personal Spend Smart goals. We suggest these goals include two perspectives:

Perspective 1 – Why _Should_ you Spend Smart?

This perspective includes all the possibilities Spend Smart offers. This is the general perspective of what Spend Smart can mean for the typical person. Some of this information will already be familiar to you. Open your mind however – the possibilities of what you can achieve with Spend Smart are beyond most people's wildest dreams. Our hope is to really stretch your thinking and challenge you to "aim high" when we talk about the second perspective…

Perspective 2 - Why do _YOU_ want to spend smart?

This really is the most important perspective. Why are you reading this book? What do you hope to get out of it. If your wildest dreams concerning your financial future could come true by following Spend Smart, what would they be?

So let's get started learning about the Whys…WHY SHOULD YOU SPEND SMART?

WHY SPEND SMART? – REASON ONE

Sometimes Spend Smart thinking goes against much of what we have heard or learned before. For example, we've all heard that the way to get ahead in life financially is to invest our money. While we agree that investing is important to financial success, the reality is that…

Spending actually has far more impact on our financial well being than investing!

Can you guess why this would be true? Yes investing is important, but how many of us have enough money at the end of the month to begin investing or consistently invest? All the information in the world about investing won't help us one bit if we don't have the money to invest. So how do we get the extra money to invest? How is spending related to investing and financial success?

HOW WE SPEND OUR MONEY DETERMINES HOW MUCH WE HAVE TO INVEST!

Most people invest less than 5% of what they earn. The current average savings (investment) rate in the US is less than one half of one percent of income. That means for every $100 earned, the typical American, invests 50 cents! What happens to the rest of the money? $99.50 of every $100.00 earned gets spent! (Sometimes people spend even more than they earn through the use of credit.)

IF WE DON'T SPEND OUR MONEY THOUGHTFULLY, WE'LL NEVER BE ABLE TO SERIOUSLY BEGIN INVESTING!

Spending is what is done with the virtually all of what we earn. If there is one thing most of us are good at it's spending! Now of course, we earn money for the purpose of buying the things we need and want. You can say money is earned for the purpose of spending, but how we spend our money affects our lives in many ways.

- If we spend all our money on "stuff", it is gone forever. We will never have be able to build up extra money for when we retire. Many people today must continue to work until the day they die because they have spent all their money – they have not used Spend Smart to keep more of what they earn. Unfortunately, not only can we spend all of our money, but we can spend more money than we have!

- If we borrow money or use credit to spend, we are giving away our future income so we can have what we want now! Some people give so much of their future income away by using credit that they never can catch up. These are the people who go bankrupt.

There is one thing the wealthy and financially secure do better than the rest of us. Its a simple idea, that we all are aware of, but tough to do…

WEALTHY PEOPLE DON'T SPEND EVERYTHING THEY MAKE! THEY LIVE BENEATH THEIR MEANS.

Financially secure people take a little bit of everything they earn and set it aside. They don't spend this money they set aside. They put this extra money to work for them by investing. This leads us to our second reason why you should Spend Smart.

WHY SPEND SMART? – REASON TWO

Spend Smart is about getting past all the myths and confusion about financial success. We want to help you create a plan for achieving your financial goals that not only imitates what other successful people have done, but also is simple enough to understand and follow so that everyone can do it. Regardless of how easy it is however, the reality of "Why You Should Spend Smart" is pretty simple – Folks, if you want to get ahead in life, you really don't have a choice…

SPEND SMART IS THE ONLY WAY FOR MOST AMERICANS TO GET AHEAD!

Here's another Spend Smart perspective that goes against what we've always heard, conventional wisdom, but the proven truth is…

YOU CAN'T EARN YOUR WAY TO FINANCIAL SECURITY.

Wow – talk about a slap in the face of the American Dream. I had always thought that financial security was all about working hard, getting raises and promotions over the years. As long as you make enough money, you'll become financially sure right? Think about this however…

- Has your income increased over the last five years?

  For most of us, the answer is yes; we are making more money than we ever have in our life.

- As your income has increased, have your expenses increased as well?

  Again, for most of us, the answer is yes. Though we are making more money than ever our expenses are also more than ever.

- SO has earning more made it easier to achieve financial security?

  DO you have more money left over at the end of the month? Are you able to invest more money in your retirement account? Even if the answer to these questions is yes, be real honest with yourself for a minute – do you have as much money left at the end of the month as you want? Are you investing enough so you will be able to retire the way you want?

Now we aren't saying that earning isn't important…we're just saying that concentrating only on what you earn will not guarantee financial security. We all have seen examples of this:

- You hear about the lottery winners who file bankruptcy a few years later.
- You know people who get a big inheritance but blow it all and soon are back to living paycheck to paycheck.
- *The Millionaire Next Door* gives examples of people who are making $750,000 a year but can't afford to retire.

The only certain way to become financially secure is by investing a little of everything that you earn…

This leads us to the third reason why you should Spend Smart…

WHY SPEND SMART? – REASON THREE

We know we should invest our money to get ahead. The difficulty is that we also know that we usually don't have any money left over at the end of the month. So how can we invest?

> **SPEND SMART CAN HELP YOU "FIND" THE MONEY FOR INVESTING, EVEN IF YOU'VE NEVER BEEN ABLE TO DO SO BEFORE!**

Financial advisors tell us the ideal amount of our income to invest is *at least* 10%. However, this rarely happens. Why don't we invest? Most of us believe "I don't invest because I can't afford to invest" - RIGHT?

Fair enough, but I want to warn you in advance. We're going to show you that this isn't a reason at all - it's just a comforting thought we use to reassure ourselves that we're doing "okay". It's funny how in polls about consumer confidence, people are confident about their future but are worried about their neighbors and friends. It is painful to face up to the reality that we are not currently on the path that will lead us to financial security.

You need to face the REALITY of why we don't invest - by the end of this book you will see hundreds of Spend Smart strategies for saving money on spending. These strategies will teach you how to end up with extra money in your pocket at the end of the month. This means you will have money for investing, even if you never did before.

Spend Smart is all about choices, however. You don't have to use your Spend Smart savings for investing if you don't want to. Regardless of what you want to do with your Spend Smart savings, if you choose not to use Spend Smart to "find" extra money, then the your reason for not achieving financial success will be a matter of personal choice, not a matter of personal finances.

WHY SPEND SMART? – SUMMARY

Why should you Spend Smart? Why should you follow what we teach in this course?

> **SPENDING IS THE AREA OF YOUR FINANCES THAT YOU CAN DO SOMETHING ABOUT RIGHT NOW, HAVE THE MOST CONTROL OVER AND MAKE THE BIGGEST IMPACT.**

For most of us, if we don't control spending we will not be able to invest. Period - it's our only hope for financial freedom. You have to stop just hoping that someday you will have enough money to start investing. Spending is the only area that you can work on now to guarantee a secure financial future. It is only by controlling spending that you have money left over to invest or to do the things you've always wanted to do, but haven't had the money for.

We have been taught to think things would be better if I could only make more money. Our experience however tells us that more income doesn't guarantee financial success. Most of us are making more than ever before in our lives, and things are still the same, or worse. You can't <u>earn</u> your way to financial security and you can't <u>earn</u> your way to wealth and you can't <u>earn</u> your way to happiness. The only sure way to get ahead is by saving some of everything you make. And Spend Smart can help you do this, regardless of your income.

Consider this challenge: Over the next 12 months, could you spend exactly the same amount of money that you make?

Your income varies:
- Will your salary go up this year, will there be overtime?
- Will you lose your job?
- Will you receive a tax refund or any other unexpected cash?

Your expenses vary as well:
- Will the car need a new transmission?
- Do you want to take a vacation?
- Will the kids need braces?

Now, can you make sure your expenses match your income to the penny? The challenge is daunting. Not even the best financial manager in the best business would try this without a cash reserve for a cushion. It would be too stressful.

Yet, each year, that is exactly how most of us approach our finances. We spend everything (if not more with credit) we make. The end result is a lot of stress, and usually we end up a little further in the hole than we were the year before. As in the business world, we need a financial plan to follow. This plan must have a specific destination with specific goals.

We need goals and a plan so we can move ahead from just barely getting by and making minimum payments, to a place where we actually start having more money than month to finally seizing total control of our finances so we will never worry about money again. That is financial independence.

With Spend Smart, you can begin the journey to financial freedom. We can show you how in as little as 5-7 years you can completely change your financial picture. You can go from paying out thousands in interest charges each year to earning enough interest on your investments to live on.

Gaining control of your financial future has many positive side effects:

OK, that's step one. You've identified a compelling reason or set of reasons about why you want to Spend Smart. This is the first step in the goal-setting process. However, you don't yet have a goal. We need to work on that next.

You have identified why you want to Spend Smart, but that's just a reason. Now we're going to take that reason and turn it into a goal. It is the intention of Spend Smart to give you all the tools necessary with this book to actually begin to accomplish everything we cover beginning today! To do so, you must have a powerful goal to fuel your action! Let's spend a little time looking at why goals are important. Hopefully this will encourage you to do a thorough job setting your goals. Then we will take your "Why I'm here" statement and turn it into a goal.

To be successful with Spend Smart you need to have a goal that you are willing to ENTHUSIASTICALLY COMMIT TO. We will lead you through a powerful process of goal setting that you can apply to any area of your life.

If followed, this goal-setting process can change your life forever.

It is so important to have goals…goals are dreams with a deadline.

Most people go through life just sort of hoping that things will work out…and they always do…but not exactly the way you want them to.

Why not take control of your destiny?

If you don't know where you're going, how will you know when you get there?

You wouldn't go on a cross-country driving vacation without a map, but most of us go through life hoping that our finances and retirement will work out. Oh sure, about age 50 or 55 we start getting concerned, but by then we have missed a lot of opportunity to make great strides.

Sure, most of us have dreams, but dreams are more like fantasies - we just think about them. Your reasons written above right now are really just fantasies – and that's ok because we haven't shown you yet how to turn them into goals. Goals on the other hand are dreams with a deadline and a structured plan to accomplish them. Goals are important because they provide a structured plan to accomplish your objectives. "No wind blows in the favor of a ship without a rudder."

What can goals do for you?

In 1953 the graduating class of Yale University was surveyed, and it turned out that only 3% of the graduates had formulated financial goals for their lives and written detailed plans to achieve those goals. In 1973, twenty years later, those same people were found and surveyed. It turned out that the 3% who left college with goals, and plans to achieve those goals were worth more financially than the other 97% combined.

This is an amazing story. It shows the power of having an objective. The other 97% were just hoping things would sort of work out. Goals must be specific and have a detailed plan outlining how to accomplish them. Later, we will teach how you how construct a powerful plan for achieving your goals. Now we are simply focusing on defining the goals.

To define your goals, we have to take your reasons for wanting to Spend Smart and turn them into precise terms. You need to put your dreams in the form of a statement that is specific and measurable. Complete the information in the following box:

Spend Smart Goals – STEP 2

Next, write your reason for being here in a specific and measurable format. Specific means how much or how big. For example, use dollar amounts and time. Here are the examples from step one:

A. My goal is to find $300 dollars every month to apply to my accelerator Margin.
B. My goal is to have $50 dollars left every month after I have paid all of my bills.
C. My goal is to start saving $100 each month for my retirement.

These goals are specific and measurable.

Finish the following sentence: *My goal is to use Spend Smart to save* _100_ *dollars every* _munt_ *so that I can…*

a cceleat mayn

The most important aspect of step 2 in this goal setting process is to make sure you have a specific and measurable reason for wanting to Spend Smart. Once it is specific and includes both a time frame and dollar amount you will then be able to refer to it as a goal!

There are a number of components to well thought-out goals. Let's look at the five components we teach as part of Spend Smart. In fact, we refer use the acronym **S.M.A.R.T.** to describe the kind of good goals you need to successful. **S.M.A.R.T.** goals are...

> **S**pecific
> **M**easurable
> **A**chievable
> **R**ealistic
> **T**otal Commitment

Specific

This is the "what" of your goals, the when you'll accomplish them, the where and how you'll do it. This is the "meat" of your goals.

Measurable

You have to be able to track your progress and know when you've accomplished a goal. A goal needs to be measurable to achieve this.

You've already gone through these first two steps of goal setting. There are three more aspects you need to consider. Continuing with our acronym...

Achievable

Obviously, it is important to set your goals high. At the same time, there are some goals that are obviously impossible. Your goals need to be possible to accomplish. If they are too large, then you should break it down into smaller pieces.

Realistic

Realistic goals are similar to Achievable goals. Achievable are more long-term as in "could you ever do this". Realistic deals more with current circumstances. Goals need to be realistic considering your current situation.

Total Commitment

You have to be totally committed to achieving your goal. The goal has to be internalized. You have to desire the achievement of your goal.

You need to apply these five components of a good goal to your goals and see how they measure up. Make sure your goal or goals are **S.M.A.R.T!**

The SMART approach is the heart of our goal-setting system. As an exercise, let's apply the SMART approach to a goal many of us have… "Having a comfortable retirement." We will walk this goal through our goal-setting system as an example.

If I say my goal is to have a comfortable retirement, what's wrong here?

That isn't a goal, it's a dream! A comfortable retirement is not **S**pecific or **M**easurable. There is no need to evaluate it any further.

There are lots of questions that need to be answered before this could be turned into a goal:

How old are you now?
When do you want to retire?
How old will you be then?
How many years away is that?

LET'S SAY WE HAVE 30 YEARS UNTIL RETIREMENT.

How much money will you need?

You need to make that decision for yourself, but for the sake of this example, let's say…

YOU WANT A $50,000 ANNUAL INCOME AT RETIREMENT in 30 years.

Now the goal is SPECIFIC - A $50,000 annual retirement income in 30 years.

The second step of the SMART goal setting method is to make the goal **MEASURABLE.**

This is a pretty easy one in this case. You need to determine what amount of account value you need to generate your annual income goal. For the sake of simplicity, let's assume that your retirement investments will grow at an annual 10% rate.

So in our example, you would need to build a retirement fund of $500,000 so at 10% interest, it would pay you $50,000 per year.

Of course, if you already have some money saved, you need to figure out how much of the $500,000 it will provide. Look at the future value of a dollar chart in your workbook.

Let's say you already have $5000 in your retirement account at work, and you're planning on retiring in 30 years, at 10% interest, that $5,000 will grow to $87,247. That means you need to build an additional $413,000 in your retirement account in 30 years. You can measure the growth of your account in dollars.

Now The Goal is Measurable

We know what we want to accomplish (50K annual income at retirement in 30 years), we know how to measure it (measure it in dollars - we need $413,000). Next we need to apply the third step of our SMART goal setting system - we need to make the goal **Achievable.**

The question becomes…

How can you build a fund worth $413,000 in 30 years?

We can't achieve the goal without knowing what steps we need to take. If you need a retirement fund worth $413,000 can you all of a sudden just earn an extra $413,000? Of course not. The good news is that with 30 years of time to work with, you can beak the goal down into reasonable pieces. Look again at wealth-building chart in the workbook. In this example, look at how much you need to be investing on a monthly basis in order to build $413,000 in 30 years – you need to invest between $175 and $200 per month.

We have now made the goal achievable in smaller steps, meaning we know what we need to do on a regular basis to accomplish the goal. Now some of you may say "I don't have that money to invest". Of course, what we are going to teach you in Spend Smart is how to find money each month to invest or do with what you want. This leads us into the fourth step of the SMART goal setting System - deciding whether the goal is **REALISTIC**?

In order to decide whether your goal is realistic, you need to consider your current situation. If the amount of money you need to invest each month is 50% of your current income, then your goal probably isn't realistic. If the amount of money you need each month to achieve your goal is around 10% of your income, then once you have studied Spend Smart, it probably is realistic.

If you think the goal is realistic, that's great, you can continue with the SMART process. If you think the goal is not realistic, then you need to either change the goal or change your situation.

We encourage people to first look at how they can change their situation before they give up on a goal, on a dream.

Changing your situation, changing how much money you have left at the end of each month is what Spend Smart is all about.

The final step of the SMART goal system is to become **totally committed** to it.

In fact, the single most important component of the process is internalizing the goal. You need to feel it in your bones. You actually have to make commitments along the way: start saving money on spending so you can begin investing. These commitments can be tough because they involve changing habits. That's why internalizing them is so very important.

You can write a great Specific, Measurable, Achievable, Realistic goal and <u>never</u> take one step toward it. If you don't commit to the goal, you won't take that first step.

If you keep doing what you've always done, you're going to get the same results you've always had.

> **Spend Smart Law of Financial Insanity - Doing the same thing you've always done with your money (spending all of it) and expecting different results (financial success).**

Most goals require a habit change - these <u>especially</u> need to be internalized.

Here is how you can internalize your goal:

1. Tell others about your goal. (If you don't need their support and think they won't be supportive - don't.) This is a public declaration - ask them to ask you how it's going periodically. It makes you accountable.
2. Fill out the goal statement in this book and post it on your bathroom mirror - read it every morning and every night. Have it at work and read it there too.

3. Every night envision yourself having already accomplished the goal. How you'll feel, what you'll do. Close your eyes and daydream about it.
4. Work your plan and reward yourself at specific points along the way.

Summary

Now that we've walked through an example of using the SMART goal system, it's time to apply it to your reasons for wanting to Spend Smart.

Review the goal statement you wrote in step 2 above. Is it Specific and Measurable? Have you broken it into bite size chunks so it is achievable? Do you have to change some things (perhaps learn Spend Smart?) to make it achievable? Are you willing to make a total commitment to it?

That is the quick run through goal setting with the SMART system. You will be using your goal statement throughout Spend Smart as you develop your specific Spend Smart plan. This goal statement will be your motivation.

Think about it everyday and do something toward achieving it by following the plan you have developed. Some people confuse other things with goals. If it's not written down, then **SMART** is a dream or a wish. A vague desire without a plan to execute is not a goal and most likely won't happen. Wishes and dreams without plans very seldom come true.

We encourage you to further refine your goal statement once you finish this book. When you have a better idea of the wealth of possibilities Spend Smart can offer, you may even come up with additional goals.

We are going to take an in-depth look at specific spending categories. You will see and decide how much you can save in each area. Every time you find a way to save with Spend Smart, you will be taking another step towards accomplishing your goals. Remember, your goals are the gasoline that will make your Spend Smart engine roar like a lion!

Congratulations on taking the first important step with Spend Smart. You now have a target to shoot for – you now have a goal. The next steps are to figure out how you are going to achieve that goal – what can you learn from Spend Smart to help you hit your target? Read on valiant Spend Smart scholar!

CHAPTER THREE
The Value of a Dollar

One dollar. A buck. A George Washington. Eight bits. A greenback. We have so many different terms for a dollar that it must be very confusing to someone learning English. These different terms highlight a problem most of us face when we make a commitment to Spend Smart. <u>We don't fully understand the value of a dollar</u>. Worse than that, we UNDERESTIMATE THE VALUE OF A DOLLAR.

That's a shame because if more people understood the value of a dollar the financial stress level in families would be greatly decreased; there would be far fewer bankruptcies; more people could enjoy their retirement instead of scraping to get by. You see, different dollars have different values. The more you can focus on getting and keeping the most valuable dollars (and the less you worry about other dollars), the more fantastically successful you can be with Spend Smart!

Please re-read that last paragraph again as it probably doesn't make much sense yet – but it will. By the time you finish this chapter you will have begun to understand the value of a dollar in a way that can change your financial future. The concept of THE VALUE OF A DOLLAR is the rocket fuel that will keep your Spend Smart program running at top speed.

Remember, earlier we talked about how changing your thinking, looking at things from a different perspective is about 60% of what it takes to be successful with Spend Smart. Understanding the value of a dollar is a large part of this change. Let's first look at the way we value a dollar at different times in our lives and how our perception of the value of a dollar changes as well.

Remember when you were a kid? What was the value of a dollar to you then? How did you measure it? Allow me a personal example. I know for me, a dollar's value was measured by how much candy I could buy! On Saturday mornings, I would sneak into Mom's purse and snatch a few dimes, or if I was lucky, I would grab a quarter or two. Then I would go to the corner store with friends and buy enough candy, gum and fun stuff to keep us busy until lunch time (this wasn't that long ago – late 60's early 70's). In fact, the value of a dollar in my mind was huge because I rarely had one.

How about when you got a little older and started earning money? What was the value of a dollar to you then? I remember the first time I got a "job", working on a farm. I would "pick rocks" all day, hard, back-breaking physical work (of course, we got a nice midday break when we were fed a huge farmer's lunch of fried chicken with mounds of mashed potatoes and rich country gravy). I was paid however the handsome sum of one dollar a day! Of course I was living high. A favorite pastime then was playing pinball at the local country store/gas station/restaurant/tavern. My value of dollar was defined by the amount of pinball I could play. I would ride my bike to the Popple Creek store, take out my dollar, have a soft-drink and could play pinball for an hour or more (depending on how many games I won at a cost of three games for a quarter).

Later when I got older, my pay rose to a dollar an hour. Of course, with increased pay, I had increased responsibilities. Now I had to milk the cows, but I had more dollars, more often. Looking back, I realize that as the number of dollars I had increased, I VALUED THEM LESS and began spending them more frivolously. Things like paying my siblings to do my chores, etc.

When I got into high school and college, my income grew as I began to earn several dollars an hour. My purchases grew as well. Ten dollars meant a lot to me because I could fill the gas tank, buy a pair of jeans or go on a date. A buck didn't mean as much because I couldn't buy much of what was important to me.

Today, as full-time income earners, our earnings are probably higher than they have ever been. Of course, the price tag of the things most important to us is much higher than previously in our life. Our most important expenses are things like a car, a mortgage payment, a family vacation, etc. A dollar really doesn't seem to have much value anymore does it? Especially compared to the value we placed on it in our earlier years.

It is time to make a change in your life – a change in your perspective. The purpose of our trip down memory lane was to highlight a point. The value of a dollar changes for people over time. It is influenced by factors such as your income, your purchases and others. In fact, THE VALUE OF A DOLLAR really IS WHATEVER YOU THINK IT IS. More to the point, the value of a dollar is WHATEVER YOU DECIDE IT IS. It depends on your perspective. And you need to make a decision right now to better your financial life by changing your perspective.

THREE VALUES OF A DOLLAR

Students of Spend Smart learn there are different ways of looking at the value of a dollar. Believe it or not, YOU ACTUALLY CAN CHANGE THE VALUE OF A DOLLAR, depending on how you decide to look at it. The value of a dollar is determined by your point of view.

Spend Smart encourages you to look at the value of a dollar in three different ways. This approach will help you improve your financial situation. The three important values of a dollar can be summarized as follows:

Purchase Value

> Purchase value refers to the value of something you can buy right now. Like candy in the earlier story, what is something you can purchase worth to you? The PURCHASE VALUE of a dollar is the value of a purchase.

Replacement Value

> Replacement value refers to the cost of replacing a dollar you spend. If you spend a dollar right now, how much will you have to work, how much will you have to earn to replace it? The REPLACEMENT VALUE of a dollar is the amount of money you must earn to replace a dollar you spend.

Future Value

Future value refers to the value of a dollar at some time in the future. If you take a dollar and invest it, what will it be worth to you? The FUTURE VALUE of a dollar is the amount of money it can grow to if invested.

Let's look at these values of a dollar more closely.

PURCHASE VALUE

The purchase value of a dollar is equal to whatever an intended purchase is worth to you. Since you value some purchases more than others and you probably value certain purchases differently than someone else would, it's easy to see that the purchase value of a dollar is very subjective. It depends on who is buying what and what the item is worth to them.

Purchase value is not a constant. It changes depending upon the item being purchased. The purchase value of a dollar becomes the value of whatever you buy with the dollar.

For example, a $20 tank of gas may be worth more to you than a $20 bouquet of flowers because you need gas in your car to get to work. SO even though the price is the same, in this example, the purchase value of a dollar is different.

The purchase value of an item also can vary from one person to another. For example, that same $20 bouquet of flowers may (at least for a short time) be worth more than the $20 tank of gas to someone who is trying to impress a date.

SPEND SMART TIP – One of the objectives of Spend Smart is to help you re-focus your spending, to spend smart. If you can spend smart on some items, you'll have more money to use for those things most important to you (the items on your Spend Smart goals list for example) RIGHT? If you start doing this, right now, TODAY, won't your financial life begin improving IMMEDIATELY?

One good way to help you spend smart is to think about the purchase value of dollar. For example, you might be walking through a store and suddenly see a super-gizmo VCR on sale for $100. Before Spend Smart, you might just automatically whip out your credit card and grab that hot deal. If you stop for a moment however and remember that one of your Spend Smart goals is to buy your next car with cash, you might realize that a car is worth more to you than the VCR. If you compare the purchase value of the dollars you buy a car with to the purchase value of the dollars you buy a VCR with, do you think you might put the VCR back on the shelf? DO you think understanding the purchase value of a dollar might help you achieve your Spend Smart goals faster?

Thinking of the purchase value of a dollar is something we all do naturally at time, but the key to financial success is consistency. Wealth and financial security is created slowly over time, like the way a small river eventually created the Grand Canyon. If you let the purchase value of a dollar be a consistent tool in your Spend Smart habits, you will have a powerful weapon in your fight for financial security.

REPLACEMENT VALUE

The replacement value of a dollar is equal to the amount of money you must earn in order to replace a dollar you spend. When you spend a dollar, you are going to have to replace that dollar – otherwise you eventually will run out of dollars!

How do you replace your dollars you spend? By going to work and earning a paycheck! Now typically we think, no big deal, I spend my $1000 or $2000 dollars this month – I'll earn that much next month. A common mistake many of us make however is to assume that the dollar in our wallet or purse is the same as a dollar we earn. Listen closely…

A DOLLAR IN YOUR POCKET IS WORTH MUCH MORE THAN A DOLLAR YOU EARN!

In fact…

A DOLLAR YOU SAVE WITH SPEND SMART IS THE MOST VALUABLE DOLLAR YOU HAVE!

How can that be. Didn't Ben Franklin tell us "a penny saved is a penny earned"? With all due respect to Mr. Franklin – HE'S WRONG. It's not his fault though. When Ben was alive we didn't have personal income tax.

Income tax is what makes the replacement value of a dollar such an important concept to understand. It's simple really. Like we said, if you spend a dollar you can replace it by earning more dollars right? The important question is how many dollars must you earn to replace a dollar? Isn't it more than a dollar?

If you earn a dollar, after taxes are taken out, you have less than a dollar. Therefore, you have to earn more than a dollar to end up with a dollar in your pocket. Financial experts like to talk about "before tax" and "after tax" money.

Spend Smart doesn't require this kind of financial rocket science. To keep it simple, just remember (AS IF YOU COULD FORGET!) that your earnings have taxes taken out. You never end up with as many dollars in your pocket as you earn. Dollars already in your pocket, don't have any (more) income taxes taken out. Spend Smart helps you keep more dollars in your pocket – and DOLLARS IN YOUR POCKET ARE THE MOST VALUABLE DOLLARS YOU HAVE.

How much more valuable are the dollars in your pocket? It depends on the amount of money you earn. It depends on what your federal and state income tax rates are. Review the following chart and find the column with your federal tax rate.

Know the Value of a Dollar!

"A penny saved is a penny earned" *--Benjamin Franklin*

Mr. Franklin had the good fortune of living in the day when there wasn't a personal income tax. His thought is not entirely true today. If he lived today his quote would be: " A dollar saved is (at least) a dollar and forty cents earned."

The following table outlines how much income you must earn to replace a dollar that you spend. In other words what is each dollar you save worth to you in earnings.

1998 Federal Tax Rates

Federal Income Tax	15.00%	28.00%	31.00%	36.00%	39.60%
State Income Tax	6.50%	6.50%	6.50%	6.50%	6.50%
Social Security Tax	6.20%	6.20%	6.20%	6.20%	6.20%
Medicare Tax	1.45%	1.45%	1.45%	1.45%	1.45%
Total Income Tax	29.15%	42.15%	45.15%	50.15%	53.75%
Replacement Value of $1	**$1.41**	**$1.73**	**$1.82**	**$2.01**	**$2.16**

Though state income tax rates vary according to state and income level, for the purpose of simplicity, an average state income tax rate of 6.5 is used. Also, even though Social Security tax is not collected on any earnings beyond $68,400, for the sake of simplicity, this chart includes Social Security tax on all income.

What is your Replacement Value of a dollar? Find it! If you are in the 15% tax bracket, the replacement value of a dollar for you is $1.41! This means that for each dollar you spend, you must earn $1.41 to replace it. More importantly…

WITH SPEND SMART, EACH DOLLAR YOU SAVE ON SPENDING, EACH DOLLAR YOU KEEP IN YOUR POCKET IS WORTH $1.41 OF EARNINGS.

Why is this? Each dollar you save is $1.41 you don't have to earn or $1.41 of earnings you can use for something else. Are you starting to understand why dollars in your pocket are the most valuable dollars you can have? Figure out what the Replacement Value of a dollar is for you and use this powerful tool to help you Spend Smart!

For the Mathematically Curious - HOW DO YOU FIGURE?

Math with percentages can be tricky. For example, if you have a dollar, and you lose a quarter, you now have 25% less money. On the other hand, if you have 75 cents and you find a quarter, you now have 33% more money.

When you look at the chart with the Replacement Value of a dollar, for those of you who aren't accountants, you might think the calculations are wrong. For example, in the first column, someone who pays 15% federal income tax, 6.5 state income tax and the regular social security and medical taxes, the total income tax is 29.15%.

If the total tax is 29.15%, how can the replacement value be $1.41 – that seems like more than 29.15%! Wouldn't the replacement value be $1.29? That's 29% more! Try the math.

Our objective is to find out how much you have to earn to have a dollar left after 29% is deducted for taxes. 29% of $1.29 is 37 cents. So if you earn $1.29, you subtract 37 cents and have 88 cents left. So the replacement value of a dollar in this example is more than $1.29.

If you earn $1.41, 29% of $1.41 equals 41 cents. Hence, if you earn $1.41 you'll subtract 41 cents for taxes and have $1.00. The Replacement Value of a dollar (assuming total income taxes of 29%) is $1.41 because that's what you need to earn in order to have a dollar left after taxes.

If you want to figure your own Replacement Value of a dollar using different tax rates, the formula is as follows:

Replacement Value = $\dfrac{1}{(1 - \text{tax \%})}$

NOTE: Tax % needs to be in decimal format, that is, 29% should be .29

Let's look at how the Replacement Value of a dollar is related to the Purchase Value of a Dollar.

How Does this affect the Purchase Value of a Dollar?

Let's say you purchase a new washer and dryer for $1000.00 (and you are in the 15% tax bracket) *You need to earn $1501.65 to buy that washer and dryer:*

Earn $1410.00 to cover the cost of the item ($1000.00)
Earn $ 91.65 to cover the cost of the sales tax ($65.00 at 6.5%)
      $1501.65 is what you need to earn to purchase that $1000 washer and dryer!

Talk about a powerful way of looking at things. Did you ever stop to think that the $1000 purchase costs you $1531.65 in earnings? Of course, the 15% tax rate is the lowest rate. If you aren't in the lowest tax bracket, that washer and dryer cost you even more in earnings!

While we hope the replacement value of dollar helps you begin to change your thinking on spending, more importantly, we hope the Replacement Value of a dollar helps you place much greater value on the dollars in your pocket. Spend Smart helps you keep more of the most valuable dollars you have.

Let's take it one step further. You're beginning to see how dollars you save are worth much more than dollars you earn. The washing machine example we used above actually under-estimates the reality of purchasing a washer and a dryer for many Americans. Many people don't make large purchases with cash. They use credit.

It gets worse you use credit to buy the washer and dryer: If you are in the 15% tax bracket, *You need to earn $1974 to buy that washer and dryer!*

Earn $1410.00 to cover the cost of the item. ($1000.00)
Earn $ 91.65 to cover the cost of sales tax ($65.00 at 6.5%)
Earn $ 472.35 to cover the cost of the interest ($ 335.00 - 12% for 5 years)
      $1974.00 is what you need to earn to purchase that $1000 washer & dryer on credit!

If someone wants to buy that washer and dryer and they don't have the $1000 cash to make the purchase, our "gotta have it now" society encourages people to use credit. When you do this, suddenly that $1000 washer and dryer now costs you $1974.00 in earnings!

Can you guess what kind of dollars actually decrease the purchase value of a dollar? Credit dollars! Think about it. When you buy the washer and dryer with cash, each dollar's worth of washer and dryer costs $1.50 in earnings. When you buy the washer and dryer on credit, each dollar's worth of washer and dryers costs $1.97 in earnings!

FUTURE VALUE

The Future Value of a dollar refers to the value of a dollar that earns interest as it grows over time. While Future Value is an investment term, remember, we don't deal with rocket science in Spend Smart. The Future Value of a dollar is an especially important concept to understand however, if you, like many people, want to begin or increase your retirement savings as one of your Spend Smart goals.

The Future Value of a dollar always depends on two factors – Interest rate and time. The Future Value of a dollar gets larger as the interest rate increase and/or the amount of time gets longer. If you know the interest rate and you know the length of time, you can calculate the Future Value of a dollar.

Let's look at an example of the Future Value of a Dollar. If you invest $1000 for 15 years and it earns 10% interest, that $1000 will grow to $4450. The Future Value of a dollar, of each dollar in this example, is $4.45

That's the financial explanation of the Future Value of a dollar. What does this mean to you and what does this mean for Spend Smart? Look at the table below to see the Future Value of a dollar at different interest rates and over different lengths of time:

Future Value of a Dollar

Number of Years

		5 years	10 years	15 years	20 years	25 years	30 years	35 years	40 years
	6%	$1.35	$1.82	$2.45	$3.31	$4.46	$6.02	$8.12	$10.96
	8%	$1.49	$2.22	$3.31	$4.93	$7.34	$10.94	$16.29	$24.27
Rate of	10%	$1.65	$2.71	$4.45	$7.33	$12.06	$19.84	$32.64	$53.70
Return	12%	$1.82	$3.30	$6.00	$10.89	$19.79	$35.95	$65.31	$118.65
	14%	$2.01	$4.02	$8.07	$16.18	$32.45	$65.08	$130.53	$261.80
	16%	$2.21	$4.90	$10.85	$24.02	$53.17	$117.72	$260.60	$576.92
	18%	$2.44	$5.97	$14.58	$35.63	$87.06	$212.70	$519.68	$1,269.70

Figure out what the Future Value of a dollar is for you. How many years before you want to retire? What do you estimate your rate of return (or interest rate) will be? Many people assume a 10% rate of return because that has been the long-term rate of return for the stock market during the 20th century.

This table tells us that the Future Value of a dollar increases the longer it is invested. That's simple enough to understand. Most of us understand that. Unfortunately, most of us have few if any dollars to invest. So why is the

Future Value of a dollar important to Spend Smart? It's important because…

In most cases, **THE FUTURE VALUE OF A DOLLAR IS THE GREATEST VALUE OF A DOLLAR.**

Spend Smart helps you find "extra" dollars in your current spending. This means that even if you've never had money to invest before, using Spend Smart strategies, you will now. You can now have the power of compound interest working for you instead against you (as it does with debt).

Putting It All Together

Now that you have begun to learn that…

ALL DOLLARS ARE NOT CREATED EQUAL

You have the most powerful motivating Spend Smart tool. By understanding the different values of a dollar, you can greatly increase your ability to use Spend Smart strategies. And the more you use Spend Smart strategies, the sooner (or greater) your financial success will be.

WHY ARE THE DIFFERENT VALUES OF A DOLLAR IMPORTANT? THEY ARE IMPORTANT BECAUSE THEY UNLEASH THE POWERFUL "MULTIPLIER" EFFECT OF SPEND SMART.

The multiplier effect helps you value dollars much more than you have before. When you value dollars more highly, you will use them more wisely! When you realize that each dollar you save is worth $1.41 in earnings, the value of a dollar is multiplied in your mind? When you understand how each dollar you save is worth $12.06 in retirement dollars, do you think that will motivate you more to Spend Smart than just the simple idea of saving a dollar will?

This chapter on the Value of a Dollar is the most important of all the chapters in this book. You can learn all the strategies and even begin using some of them to improve your financial situation. If you really want to achieve your goals however, if you are committed to doing what it takes to turn your dreams into reality…

YOU WILL NEED TO USE THE CONCEPT OF THE VALUE OF A DOLLAR TO ACHIEVE YOUR GREATEST SPEND SMART SUCCESS!

The key to achieving financial success is to make as many smart choices as you can, and to do it as often as you can. Consistent action creates consistent results. Don't fool yourself into thinking otherwise because…

NO SINGLE SPEND SMART STRATEGY BY ITSELF WILL MAKE YOU RICH.

You need the power of numbers, you need massive action, you need to use as many Spend Smart strategies as possible to achieve financial success. One or two Spend Smart strategies by themselves will not do the trick. Even as you get to the point where you use a large number of Spend Smart strategies…

JUST USING SPEND SMART STRATEGIES ONCE OR TWICE WILL NOT MAKE YOU RICH EITHER

Repetition is the key to success. Using a Spend Smart strategy on a regular and consistent basis will give you better and better results. When you do something often enough, it begins to become a habit. Spend Smart is a good habit to practice. Not only that, saving money with Spend Smart will have a snowball effect for you.

When you see yourself making progress towards your goals, you're going to get excited. This excitement feeds on itself. As you see results, you're going to look for more Spend Smart ideas to increase your results. It's like a snowball at the top of a hill, starting out small, starting out slowly, but gaining speed and power as it rolls down the hill.

You need to use as MANY Spend Smart ideas as often as you can to get the most from this textbook. This is the most important chapter because using what you've learned about the Value of a Dollar will motivate you to use as many Spend Smart strategies as often as you can.

The Value of a Dollar – Using it for Spend Smart Success

In teaching Spend Smart, we find that people may at first think some of the saving tips aren't very valuable. They think the money saved by following some of the strategies isn't worth their time or effort. For example, when I first began collecting Spend Smart ideas, I thought the ones that saved me less than $10 weren't worth bothering with.

I save about $9 when I change my own oil. No big deal right? When you think about the Replacement Value of a dollar however, you appreciate the value of that $9 much, much more. I am much more motivated to Spend Smart by changing my oil when I think of the Replacement Value of a dollar.

If I can save $9 by changing my own oil, that has a replacement value of $15.39. If I don't change my own oil, then $15.39 of my earnings must be used to get an oil change. When I do change my own oil however, I now have an extra $15.39 of earnings that doesn't have to be spent on an oil change.

When I Spend Smart, when I save money, I can do something else, whatever I want with that $15.39 of earnings that would have otherwise been used for an oil change. WOW – Doesn't that have the same impact on my financial situation as earning an extra $15.39? Absolutely. Like Ben Franklin said, a penny saved is penny earned (but we know it's more than a penny earned). That's the power of the Replacement Value of a dollar.

Saving on spending, using Spend Smart strategies is similar to having another job or source of income. You should think of Spend Smart that way because it makes more money available to you than you would have otherwise had. It's another source of dollars just like a job is. And this is the best "job" you'll ever have.

With Spend Smart, you don't have to commute, you can "work" at Spend Smart whenever you want and best of all, no income taxes are taken from the money you save. If you had a second job, you would have additional dollars to use you how want right? Think of Spend Smart as an additional source of dollars and you're success will grow.

Using the Future Value of a dollar can be a very motivating Spend Smart tool as well. Many of the ideas in this book will save you $1 or less. You can understand that for many people that probably doesn't excite them very much!

If you save $1 in spending, you now have the opportunity to invest that dollar. For the typical American, the Future Value of that dollar is $12.06 in retirement dollars. Now saving just $1 may not get you excited, but does the idea of an extra $12.06 at least get your interest?

SUMMARY

Studies show that most people do not achieve the financial success in life they had hoped for. In fact, at age 65, 96% of people have incomes under $35,000 per year. If you do what these people do – if you think like they do – don't you think there's a good chance you'll have the same results?

If you want to succeed financially, Spend Smart is the place to start. 60% of your success at Spend Smart will be based on your ability to change your thinking. The concept of the value of a dollar is the cornerstone to changing you thinking about money. Use the Value of a Dollar to propel your Spend Smart success.

If you make Replacement Value and Future Value a regular part of your thought process every time you spend money, fantastic things will start to happen in your financial life. First, you will spend much less on things you don't really want or need. Second, you will make better spending decisions on the things that you really do need.

Next time you're driving by McDonald's and consider going through the drive-through for that $3.29 Big Mac extra value meal, think about the Future Value of a dollar. Is that Big Mac really worth $39.67 (Future Value of a dollar - $12.06) in retirement dollars to you?

Next time you see a pair of shoes that catches you attention, think about the Replacement Value of a dollar. They might be a great deal at $73.48 ($69 plus tax) but are they really worth $103.60 (Replacement Value of a dollar - $1.41) in earnings to you?

Now that you understand the different values of a dollar you have a better basis for making better spending decisions, for using Spend Smart. Start thinking about and using the Value of a Dollar whenever you buy something. You may feel silly at first, but who cares? It takes practice and repetition to be successful at anything.

A great eastern philosopher said, "the journey of 1000 miles begins with the first step". Take that first step, then the second, and start on your way. While the journey to financial success is long and challenging, changing your thinking about the Value of a Dollar will help you follow the Spend Smart path. And if you become a champion at Spend Smart, you can achieve all of your financial dreams.

CHAPTER FOUR
Plan Your Way to Spend Smart Success

Success occurs when planning and hard work come together. To succeed with Spend Smart you need a plan. You need a plan to guide you, a plan to help you know what to do and when to do it in order to maximize your Spend Smart success. As the Zen proverb tells us "The journey of 1000 miles begins with the first step". With Spend Smart, your plan will tell you what your first step (and second, third steps, etc.) should be.

When you go on a trip, do you jump in your car and just start driving? Or do you look at a map, check out different routes and then decide what roads to take? You make a plan, don't you? Do you think you are more likely to reach your destination if you have a plan or is jumping in the car without a map just as good?

Hopefully, you have spent some time creating your Spend Smart goals. This is important because your goals are your destination. Your Spend Smart goals tell you where you want to go. How can you start your journey if you don't know where you're going? (Of course, if you don't know where you're going then you don't need a map!) How will you know you've arrived if you don't know where you want to go. If you haven't already defined your Spend Smart goals, we encourage you to DO IT NOW, before continuing on.

This textbook is your road map. Using it, you will be able to understand and learn different Spend Smart Strategies to help you achieve financial success. You will look at different "routes" to your "destination" or goals. Then you will be able to choose the strategies that make you feel most comfortable and follow them to your destination. Sounds like a road trip!

Your Spend Smart plan is really a financial plan, because it involves money. This plan however is not what we usually think of as a financial plan. Traditional financial plans usually consist of an investment / insurance plan and strategy. Spend Smart however is not about investing – as you know, it's about saving money on your spending, keeping more of what you earn.

Some people are excellent planners. They put together a step by step plan of how to get from point A to point B. Other people may not plan very well, but they are great at "grabbing the bull by the horns" and taking action. Either approach will help you achieve some Spend Smart success, but to maximize your chances of success:

YOU MUST CREATE A PLAN TO SPEND SMART AS OFTEN AS POSSIBLE!

This plan is the heart of Spend Smart. Like the millionaires in *The Millionaire Next Door*, you want to create a financial plan that you will update and review on a regular basis. There is a common type of "financial plan" used by many households. This plan is called a BUDGET!

To most of us, the thought of a budget makes us cringe in pain and stick our tongues out in disgust. Budget is a word that can strike fear into the heart of even the most determined Spend Smart student. It makes us think we have to "do without" and act like a penny-pinching Scrooge. Trust us for a moment however and let's get this bad news out of the way while you consider the unique benefits of the budget we use in Spend Smart.

Using a Budget is Critical to Your Spend Smart Success

A budget is nothing more than a plan. This plan lets us know where we are, where we're going and how we're going to achieve our financial goals. The good news however is that Spend Smart includes a unique type of budget where you don't have to track every penny you spend. This budget is called the REVERSE BUDGET. The Reverse Budget will be the easiest budget you've ever seen but it will also put money in your pocket!

If you've read popular "financial management" books, then you certainly know the benefits of having a traditional household budget. *The*

Millionaire Next Door teaches us that one of the most common traits among millionaires is the fact that they create and follow a monthly budget. If your parents or grandparents lived through the depression era, they probably were excellent "budgeting" role models. When you see "investment experts" on TV, they talk about making a budget and including 10% of your income for yourself. They tell you what to do but they don't tell you how to do it. Spend Smart teaches you how to "find" that 10% for yourself!

All of our lives, we've been bombarded by this message about the importance of budgeting. So, since society has been nagging us about budgeting for years, we've all got a detailed household budget that we use each month, right? Wrong! Even though it easier than ever to create and maintain a traditional budget with software like Quicken or Microsoft Money, less than 5% of US households create and use a detailed monthly budget.

What's the resistance? We've heard all the reasons why we should have a budget. We know what it can do for us. We've heard all the "conventional wisdom" from the financial gurus about how to create a budget. So why don't we do it?

PEOPLE DON'T USE BUDGETS BECAUSE BUDGETS TAKE TOO MUCH WORK.

It is human nature to take the "path of least resistance" or to take the easy way out. A common attitude is we don't need to bother with budgets if we are paying our bills. Doing a budget takes time and most of us are already stretched too thin for time (maybe it's because we have to work so hard to pay our bills?) We have other "priorities". We don't have time to do a budget. Spend Smart offers a solution with the Reverse Budget:

THE REVERSE BUDGET TAKES ONLY A FRACTION OF THE TIME THAT A "TRADITIONAL BUDGET" TAKES.

The reality of the situation tells us that time isn't the only reason people avoid doing a budget like the plague. Most of us would do almost anything (within reason of course) if the money is right. The reason we don't take the time to do a budget is that we don't know how much it is worth to us. We don't see a specific dollar amount that a budget can put in our pockets. We don't know what a budget can mean to our financial situation.

THE REVERSE BUDGET MOTIVATES YOU BECAUSE IT TELLS YOU EXACTLY HOW MUCH MONEY IT WILL PUT IN YOUR POCKET.

Traditional budgets are focused on one specific task – tracking spending. Some people take this to the extreme and carry a little notebook to write down everything they spend from small items like a cup of coffee or lunch, to regular expenses like the electric bill or the mortgage, to the "surprise" expenses like dental bills or car repairs. Now if you have the discipline to track every penny you spend, I guarantee you will naturally begin to spend less money. Spend Smart takes an easier path however. With the Reverse budget, tracking all expenses is not required.

THE REVERSE BUDGET TRACKS ONLY THE MONEY YOU SAVE!

The following table compares the Reverse Budget to traditional budgets:

Traditional Budget	Reverse Budget
• Track all Spending	• Track Savings Only
• Many Changes each Month	• Only a Few Changes each Month
• No Specific Dollar Value	• Exact Dollar Value

With the Reverse Budget, you don't budget for spending. You budget for savings. The best part is:

YOU DECIDE HOW MUCH MONEY YOU ARE GOING TO SAVE!

This means you simply plan which Spend Smart Strategies you are going to use. The budget portion is simply tracking the money you save with each strategy and totaling your savings.

You have probably noticed that many of the Spend Smart Strategies described throughout this book include a specific dollar amount that the typical person or household can save by using. These specific dollar savings figures are important because they help you place a value on the strategy. It helps you decide if it is worthwhile, in terms of dollars and cents whether a certain strategy is worth following for you.

Other strategies don't have a specific savings amount because they vary greatly depending on you and how often you use a product or how much you use. With these strategies, it is useful for you to estimate how much the strategy will save you. Don't be afraid to be conservative or liberal with your estimates. Again, do what is comfortable for you – make an estimate you feel comfortable with.

It's important to have a dollar amount associated with each Spend Smart Strategy you use. That way, you can include it with your Reverse Budget. Take a look at the Reverse Budget form on the following page:

Category	Item	Strategy	Annual Savings
Appliances	*Washing Machine*	*Use cold water (10 loads per week)*	*$104*
Automobile	*Oil Change*	*Learn to do it myself*	*$80*
Debt	*Credit Cards*	*Negotiate a lower interest rate*	*$500*
Groceries	*Cereal*	*2 boxes Store Brand Cereal / week*	*$100*
Insurance	*Auto*	*Raise deductible from $250 to $500*	*$300*
Utilities	*Electricity*	*Enroll in Energy Saver Program*	*$75*

Using the Reverse Budget

To use the Reverse Budget, you simply fill in the appropriate information in the columns. To do this, you must read and review this entire book. You need to decide which Spend Smart Strategies you are going to try. Which strategies seem like they wouldn't be too difficult for you? Which ones seem like they fit your lifestyle and would be worth the effort. What are your goals and how much do you want to save on spending with Spend Smart? All of these questions help you choose the Spend Smart Strategies that are right for you?

Go through each category of Spend Smart Strategies. When you find one you would like to try, simply write down the category, item, strategy and most importantly, the annual savings. Annual savings is important because this is the exact number of dollars that Spend Smart is going to help you capture - the dollars you are going to end up with in your pocket.

You need to begin building a reverse budget for yourself. We use the word "begin" because this will be a flexible plan that let's you experiment and change things over time. Over the months ahead, you will find more strategies you want to try or you may decide that you don't like some strategies. Use the forms in the appendix and make extra copies for the future.

As suggested throughout this book, these ideas only serve as a starting point. You will become excited as you see extra dollars in your pocket each month. You will be motivated to find more ways to Spend Smart and to learn more from other sources. As you become more aware of the value of a dollar, as you become more experienced with Spend Smart, as you find other books and sources of information for new Spend Smart ideas, you will add more items to your Reverse Budget.

As a starting point, with your first Reverse Budget, don't overwhelm yourself with too many strategies right away. Maybe find ten or so ideas to use in your first month with Spend Smart. Now, it's very likely the savings from your first Reverse Budget might not reach your Spend Smart goal.

THAT'S OK – DON'T WORRY ABOUT IT!

WHEN YOU ARE IN THE FIRST FEW MONTHS OF YOUR REVERSE BUDGET, YOUR MAIN JOB IS TO FIND SPEND SMART STRATEGIES THAT "WORK" FOR YOU.

Make notes in the book as you read it when you notice a Spend Smart Strategy that has potential for you. Once you have finished reading this book, it shouldn't take more than an hour or two to pick the strategies you want to use in your first Reverse Budget.

As you go through a few months, you'll have a better idea of which ideas you like and feel comfortable with. If you find some that aren't working out for you, that's perfectly fine. Erase them from your Reverse Budget! Just make sure you add a few new strategies each month so your savings continue to grow!

Like the millionaires, remember to review your financial plan, your Reverse Budget, EACH AND EVERY MONTH. Make a commitment to yourself to do this. Set a date – schedule a time that you will stick to.

When you sit down to review your Reverse Budget, ask yourself questions. Be honest with yourself about what's working and what's not. Are you getting closer to your Spend Smart goals? Which new ideas do you want to try? Go wild! Experiment with different ideas. Find other sources for more idea (check out appendix 3 for more books, newsletters, Internet sites, etc.). Don't be afraid to try strategies, even if they seem strange.

You will not use strategies if you are not comfortable with them. The more strategies you use, the more money you save. You can only get comfortable with a strategy if you test it, if you try it out. Being comfortable will help you use your Spend Smart Strategies consistently and often.

Most importantly, you need to feel confident. Confident in your strategies and the Reverse Budget. You need to know you will use the Reverse

Budget and you need to BELIEVE IT WILL REALLY SAVE YOU MONEY. In fact, this confidence will determine how much money you will put back in your pocket each month. We'll talk more about this in the *Seize Your Savings* chapter.

Summary

To achieve your Spend Smart Goals, to get to where you want to be you need a plan. Now of course, if you just dabble in Spend Smart, apply strategies when you think of them, you will save money, but to really excel, to really change your financial future with Spend Smart, you need to have a written strategy. The Reverse Budget is this strategy.

The great motivational and self-improvement teachers teach us that success is really easier than many of us realize. They say if you want to be successful, imitate other successful people. Sounds simple, right – but first you have to know what other successful people do.

As we know from the Millionaire Next Door, financially successful people create a plan in writing, stick to it and review it on a regular basis.

IF YOU WANT TO BE SPEND SMART SUCCESSFUL, ACT LIKE A MILLIONAIRE!

The Reverse Budget is your written financial plan. You need to create it, make a personal commitment to it and use it and review it on a regular basis. If you do this simple task, you will be well on your way to Spend Smart Success. You will be on your way to the financial success you always had hoped for, but never dreamed would be possible.

CHAPTER FIVE
The Psychology of Buying

We all make purchases every day - maybe it's stopping to get gas, grabbing lunch or picking up some milk or bread on the way home. In these frequent purchasing situations, we have very a specific purpose, a very specific need.

We also have purchasing situations, usually on at least a weekly basis, where our purpose is much more general or perhaps even completely undefined. We need groceries. We need some new shoes. We have to get a gift for someone. Or maybe, we're just going to the mall.

In this section, we are going to look at the psychology of buying. Why we buy the things we do, when we do. How we can recognize the difference between what we need and what we want. If you want to learn how to Spend Smart, it is crucial to begin to understand the psychology of buying.

Let me ask you a question. Do you KNOW SOMEONE,

- Who has a two-car garage, but has to park one car in the driveway?
- Who would like to remodel their basement, but can't until they have a garage sale?
- Who has a guest bedroom, but guests sleep on the couch?

The bottom line…most of us buy much more than we need but we never can buy everything we want.

Why is this? Let's look briefly at the psychology of buying.

Anyone ever hear the story of Pavlov's dog? It demonstrates some very relevant psychological phenomena known as STIMULUS/RESPONSE and ASSOCIATION. Now I'm not implying that we are dogs, but these psychological terms can help explain why we often buy things we don't need.

The story of Pavlov's dog, basically goes like this. Pavlov noticed how the dog always salivated when he saw his dinner coming. Of course, this makes sense, right? The dog knows how good that Alpo is going to taste. The stimulus (thought of dog food) produced a response (slobbering)

So Pavlov, being a good scientist, began to wonder how strong this relationship between the stimulus and the response was. He suspected the link might be so strong, that he could substitute a different, unrelated stimulus and still produce the same response. In other words, he thought he could get the dog to salivate, **AS LONG AS HE SIMPLY THOUGHT DINNER WAS COMING!**

Pavlov decided to conduct an experiment to test his theory. He began to ring a bell right before he would bring food to the dog. Over time, the dog began to salivate when the bell was rung, even before dinner was served. In fact, **THE DOG WOULD SALIVATE ANYTIME THE BELL WAS RUNG, EVEN IF DINNER WASN'T SERVED.**

Pavlov explained this phenomena as ASSOCIATION, meaning, the dog associated the bell with dinner, so the bell produced the same STIMULUS/RESPONSE reaction. The dog expected the stimulus (dinner) and would respond (salivate) from just the bell alone because such a strong link had been created between the bell and dinner.

WHAT THE HECK DOES THIS HAVE TO DO WITH SPEND SMART?

Very simple - just like Pavlov's dog, we get our "bell" rung all the time. We are bombarded with advertisements - these advertisements create images or ASSOCIATIONS about products in our mind. What is really interesting is these images or associations often have little to do with actual product benefits. They focus on the feelings we will get from the product. They evoke emotional responses from us. Let's look at some examples of advertising where the focus is on a feeling instead of the product itself.

- Insurance commercials about happy families.
- Makeup ads showing fashion shoots.
- Beer commercials with men drinking the beer surrounded by beautiful women.
- Nike commercials featuring popular music and athletes - sometimes they don't even show the product name - just the "swoosh".
- Pickup Truck commercials featuring "tough" guys.

WHY DO THEY DO THIS?

Think back to Pavlov's dog. Advertisers want us to associate good emotional feelings with their product, the stimulus. They want us to buy the product, the response. Psychologically, many consumers believe they can purchase the good feelings associated with the product, so they buy it.

Advertising is about psychology because buying is often based more on emotion than on logic. If you can better understand the psychology why you do things, why you buy certain things.

NEEDS VERSUS WANTS.

Talking about the psychology of buying helps us understand why we choose certain products. Another aspect to consider however is how or why we decide to make a certain type of purchase.

What is the difference between needing something and wanting something? As we mentioned earlier, most of us really have everything we need - our basic needs are rather limited - Food, Shelter, Clothing. Our desires, the things we want, are large in number.

There are certain purchases we make that WE MUST MAKE - they are requirements. Requirements function on several levels. There are a small number of physical requirements - We physically need food, shelter and clothing because we can't survive without them. Some things we need in order to pay for our other needs. Most people need a car to get to work, white-collar workers need "work clothes", we need daycare for our kids, etc.

Everyone also has a number of purchase choices which are optional. MANY PURCHASES WE MAKE ARE NOT REQUIRED. We choose many of these items simply because WE WANT THEM. Such items may include a second or third car, multiple TV sets, or the latest computer system. We often purchase non-essential items because WE WANT THEM.

Now we don't have to tell you what things you buy are non-essential. What we want can affect required purchases as well. For example, while we may need a car to get to work, do we really need an SUV as opposed to a sedan?

Non-essential purchases can significantly impact our financial futures. We do have choices however. We can purchase a smaller amount of the things we want now or we can have a larger amount of the things we want later in life.

How can you tell the difference between NEEDING SOMETHING and WANTING SOMETHING?

It is a skill, an ability to separate yourself from the feelings and emotions of buying something, that can only be developed over time. The Spend Smart class is designed to help you become better at doing so. Here's a great tip to help you distinguish between the two. When you see something that you want, but you haven't planned on buying…

STOP and as parents like to say "take a time out". To be objective, you need to separate yourself from the buying situation. You need to get away from the influences of lights, colors and display usually found in a store. Take 24 hours to consider whether you really need the item. If after 24 hours you still feel you want it, then make your decision. More than half the time however, when you remove yourself from the emotion of the moment, you will decide you can do something better with your hard-earned money.

SPEND SMART IS NOT ABOUT TELLING YOU WHAT YOU SHOULD OR SHOULD NOT BUY. IT IS DESIGNED TO HELP YOU GET THE MOST OUT OF YOUR PURCHASING DOLLARS SO YOU CAN ACHIEVE LONG-TERM GOALS. UNDERSTANDING HOW AND WHY PURCHASING DECISIONS ARE MADE WILL CREATE AN AWARENESS THAT HELPS YOU SPEND SMART. THE MOST IMPORTANT ASPECT OF SPENDING YOU SHOULD BE AWARE OF IS THIS…

MOST PURCHASING DECISIONS ARE DRIVEN BY EMOTION

You don't buy something based on what you think…you buy something based on how you feel, based on your emotional makeup at the time. To further awareness about spending, it is important to learn about what some refer to as spending personalities.

Spending Personalities

We all have different personalities. When we meet, talk, or participate in activities with other people, our personality influences not only how others see us, but our actions as well. Our personality reflects the way we think and the way we act.

Most psychologists agree that at birth, your personality is like a blank sheet of paper. You are not born outgoing or shy, but you are influenced and shaped by the people, places and experiences in your life. These factors make an impression on you and your personality like a pencil leaves an impression on paper.

So in one sense, you are not entirely responsible for your personality. At the same time, if you choose to, you'll be pleased to know you can change your personality with time and effort. The ability to change your personality will become an important component of your growing ability to spend smart.

Now what do personalities have to do with spending? Any ideas?

It probably won't surprise you to learn that our personalities influence the way we spend as well. Author J. Grady Cash, in his 1994 book *Conquer the 7 Deadly Money Mistakes*, identifies what he calls seven Spending Personalities. These personalities are actually patterns of behavior that lead to what Cash calls spending mistakes. Bad money decisions. Spending that does not support your overall goals and objectives. The Spend Smart workshop will help you increase your good spending decisions, and decrease your bad spending decisions gradually over time.

Spending personalities can change depending on your mood (happy/sad), recent events (more money/less money) and emotions about a purchase (I hate buying groceries but I love to shop for clothes).

Many people have a primary spending personality that almost always affects their spending. People without a primary spending personality usually have a secondary spending personality that often affects their spending. In fact, some people have multiple secondary spending personalities. No, we're not talking about Sybil here, but we all have different personalities that surface at various times. This is often true with spending personalities.

If you want to influence the way you buy things, and really strive to spend smart, it is important that you understand why you do what you do, and what you can do to improve the way you do things. If you simply are able to identify your spending personality, simply become aware of it, and consciously trying to control it, will greatly help you in your efforts to spend smart! We call this the "Cholesterol Effect". When people simply become aware of the dangers of high cholesterol, it becomes less satisfying to eat unhealthy food and it can in fact, become even more satisfying to know you are getting healthier!

Now let's take a look at these seven spending personalities.

Spending Personality I - Impulse Buying

When we conduct Spend Smart workshops, we usually find the largest number of people have Impulse Buying as a primary or secondary spending personality. Even if it is not your personality, Impulse Buying is something that almost everyone is influenced by occasionally.

- Have you ever gone to pick up milk and bread at the grocery store and left with two bags full?
- Have you ever returned home to find that you spent more than you planned on a shopping trip?
- Have you ever purchased items form the racks next to the checkout counter?

Like any spending personality, Impulse Buying exists in people to varying degrees. In severe situations, impulse buying can become a habit, it can become a clinical addiction where what is bought doesn't matter - the thrill (or fix), the instant gratification, the emotional rush some people get from buying is all that matters. For most people, impulse buying is a personality that exerts itself infrequently with larger purchases or more often with smaller purchases. Don't kid yourself however...all of us buy things we don't need...even if you didn't have a high score on this personality be aware of the way impulse buying adds up quickly over time.

What causes Impulse Buying?

- Lack of planning
  If you don't have a specific, written list of what you are planning to purchase when you go shopping, how do you know when you're done (when you don't see anything else you want or when you're out of money

- Lack of clear financial priorities.
  When we are tempted with an impulse purchase, one of the ways we justify it is we can't think of anything else we want more at the moment. We don't have a goal, an objective which we are trying to save towards, so it easy to spend money you don't think "you need".

- Large "Deal Quotient".

  The deal quotient is a phenomena which impacts many buying decisions. Two variables generally determine how good a deal you perceive an item to be. First is how much we want or need something - this is the value we put on it. The second variable factor is the cost of an item.

  The deal quotient is calculated like this: VALUE/COST = DEAL Q

  Without getting into too much algebra, this equation basically tells you what you already know - the more you want or value something and/or the less it costs, **THE BETTER THE DEAL!**

  These variables are subjective, not easily or consistently defined. Advertising and marketing can greatly inflating the D-Q.

  For example, automobile commercials typically promote a tough, rugged, cowboy image for those who drive pickup trucks. Did you know however, that 75% of pickup owners live in urban areas? So why do they buy pickups? For some, they have a subconscious desire to be rugged, and because of the advertising, they see a pickup as a way to be rugged. Do you think there would be so many "Urban Cowboys" without such advertising? This is an example of advertising inflating the D-Q. Ordinarily, a pickup might not be appealing to an urbanite - advertising makes some want it more so the D-Q increases.

  Marketing also can inflate the D-Q. This is especially true with regard to pricing and packaging. For example, do you think someone would perceive a cost of $18,000 to be more or less than a cost of $299/mo. Cars are again a good example - financed, per-month pricing is almost always used because people perceive the cost to be lower. If the cost is perceived to be lower, than again, the D-Q goes up!

Of course, any given item usually has different Deal Quotients for different people. Take a look at the Deal Quotient Table in your workbook. Think of the last purchase you made that was more than $20 and walk it through the Deal Quotient process. Did you get a good deal?

We provide several tools during Spend Smart workshops which will help people more objectively and rationally think through purchasing decisions. This rational process helps you break free from the emotion of buying. If you simply use these tools to analyze potential purchases, you will save by making smarter purchasing decisions and by deciding against some purchases you might have made in the past. You will master the psychology of buying.

One of the tools to help you spend smart is the Deal Quotient mentioned above. The D-Q can help you make more consistent spending decisions - it can help you look at all decisions on a common scale, with a constant perspective.

Remember that the DQ rises as value goes up and cost goes down. You should begin making the DQ a regular part of spending decisions. Before you buy something, rate it's value to you on a low to high scale of 1 to 10. Rate it's cost on a low-to-high scale of 1 to 10. Check the DQ (if you're not quick with division in your head, use the workbook chart as a reference.)

With items that you purchase frequently (food, clothing, etc.) you will soon know their DQs intuitively. On items you purchase less frequently (electronics, furniture, automobiles, etc.) you will find the DQ to be an important component of your decision.

Looking again at the table in your workbook, you see the DQ can range from .10 to 10. It is important to establish some personal parameters as to what DQs you find acceptable. For example, you probably wouldn't want to buy something with a DQ less than 1 - this means that you rated the cost as being higher than the value. In other words, you would be paying more than it is worth, certainly not a good Spend Smart strategy.

Many businesses use the 2 times rule as a general guide to pricing, that is, they need to sell something for twice what they paid for it in order to cover overhead and make a reasonable profit. If someone wanted to apply this rule to personal spending, a purchase would need to have a DQ of 2 or higher (value is at least twice the cost). We have shaded the chart on page 3 for easy reference in applying the 2 times rule - ¼ of all the DQ ratios show a purchase decision where the value is twice the cost. It is these kind of winning decisions which can fuel your spend smart plan!

We do recognize that there are situations when value or price are of no object. If it's 3 AM and you're out of diapers, you probably don't care if they cost twice as much at Super America than they do at Target (thus the DQ is one-half of what it would be at Target). If you get a flat in the middle of a rainstorm and you have to walk to a service station because your spare is flat, you probably don't care if all they have are low-quality retread tires.

Use the Deal Quotient as a consistent measuring stick for knowing if your decisions are consistent with Spend Smart. This one tool can help you save a great deal of money - but now, let's continue on with spending personalities.

How can you protect against impulse buying?

- Walk Away - when you are in the physical presence of an unplanned purchase, the urge to buy is the strongest. GET OUT! Research has shown that when someone walks away from an item to "think about it", 90% of the time they do not return to buy!

- Use a Shopping List - regardless of what you are going to purchase - have a list and stick to it. Impulse buying is an emotional response - use the logic of a list to overcome the emotion. In the case of a large item purchase, have a list of the features you will purchase so you are not tempted by the little "extras".

- Carry only enough cash to make the purchase. While we advocate completely doing away with credit cards. If you still have cards, at least leave the cards (and checkbook) at home so if you are tempted you won't have convenient means for making an unplanned purchase.

- Always have a savings objective, a goal you are working towards - that way the potential pleasure of an impulse buy can be counteracted by your desire to achieve a goal.

If there is something you really feel you must have, still commit to walking away - when you get home, add the item to your list on the refrigerator of your Spend Smart goals. This guarantees you win! If something you normally would have bought on impulse, stays important over a matter of days, weeks and months then you're happy because you'll soon be able to have it. If it's importance pales as the emotions of the impulse situation fade, you've saved yourself some money - congratulate yourself on your spend smart victory!

The key to avoiding impulse buying is making it more difficult to do. You also must focus on positive reasons for not making impulse purchases. Grady Cash calls this Spending By Choice. Instead of looking at resisting impulse buying as a choice between having something or not, look at it as a choice between a gamble now (an impulse purchase) or a sure thing later (achieving one of your goals). Choose to plan your spending and you will improve your Spend Smart capabilities.

Spending Personality II - Fanatical Shopping

Do you know anyone who will drive all the way across town to save a few cents on a gallon of gas? How about someone who will go Christmas shopping at 6 AM the day after Thanksgiving because that's when the best prices can be found? If you know someone like this than you probably know a Fanatical Shopper.

Fanatical shoppers will spend huge amounts of time and effort to save any amount of money. They have a compelling desire to control money, perhaps an insecurity that they.will not have money in the future, so they see every purchase.as a win/lose proposition. There is no gray area - either you get the lowest possible price, or you lose.

The ironic thing about Fanatical Shopping is that many times, in the quest for the lowest possible price, quality and time and money spent finding the lowest price are ignored often resulting in a purchase **WHICH COSTS MORE IN THE LONG TERM.**

Fanatical Shopping can be similar to Impulse Buying, but there is a clear distinction. For example, both might buy something with a great D-Q. A Fanatical Shopper is different because they might buy something EVEN IF THEY DON'T NEED IT! - An Impulse Buyer would be less likely to do this. Fanatical Shopper can become so obsessed with saving money they may buy ridiculously larger quantities (amounts they could never use in a reasonable period of time) or more expensive items by rationalizing they are saving more money.

How can you control Fanatical Shopping?

Fanatical Shoppers already are very good at finding lowest cost items. Since they have a strong desire to save money, this desire can be easily channeled into good Spend Smart practices. Fanatical Shoppers simply need a more balanced perspective so they can better focus on satisfying their needs, not just saving money on prices.

- Consider Value and Cost - Use DQ in making purchase decisions - as we know, just because something has a low price doesn't mean it has a good DQ. If something has little or no value to you, it doesn't matter how much "money you save" on the purchase - it's not a Spend Smart decision.

- Put a Value on your Time and other Costs - Saving money on the price is good, but be realistic about the cost of your time and other costs necessary to find the extra savings. If you spend several days to save a few bucks, is that really worth it? There are many things you can do, as discussed later in the class, to save money without shopping (preparing the week's meals on the weekend for example). Once you put a value on your time, it is easier to determine when your search of a bargain is no longer worthwhile.

- Focus on the Big Picture - there is a battle to control your spending - advertisers spend huge amounts of money to influence your purchasing, but they don't worry about any one ad changing your thinking. They simply focus on using a consistent strategy over time. You should do the same. Focus on Spend Smart strategies to maximize your savings and fun over the long term. Don't worry about occasionally missing out on a better deal - it can distract you from your goals.

Spending Personality III - Passive Buying

The old football saying "When in doubt, Punt!" applies perfectly to Passive buying. Passive Buyers don't like to shop, and usually procrastinate, often costing themselves money. For example, they may have leaking pipes, but they might not do anything about it until the leaking water has rotted out the floorboards. When Passive Buyers finally do get around to buying, they are in a huge hurry to get it over with.

Passive Buyers can be a salesperson's dream. Some have the potential to be good shoppers but feel they don't have time or don't place a high priority on saving money. They don't comparison shop and don't ask questions even if they don't understand something because they don't want to appear stupid. This lack of assertiveness can leave them vulnerable to salespeople talking them into expensive "extras" (extended warranty?) they don't need because they don't want to think about it. Of course, this behavior provides a convenient excuse if the purchase doesn't end up pleasing them. The Passive Buyer can always blame it on the salesperson instead of accepting responsibility for their own actions.

Many people at times slip into the behavior of the Passive Buyer. This happens when they are confronted with decisions where they feel uneducated. Buying a house is a good example. In fact, Passive Buying is so common when buying a house, especially with regard to not asking enough questions aspect, that you are required to sign a number of disclosure documents stating that you understand certain aspects of the transaction. This is a direct result of people being unhappy with Real Estate purchases and then blaming the real estate agent.

How can you control Passive Buying?

- Beat Procrastination by Focusing on Benefits - Keep track of good spending decisions - start a journal. Contrast your smart purchases to what you would have done as a Passive Buyer. You'll soon begin to associate positive feelings and emotions with shopping.

- Become a Student and get Paid for it - accept that there will always be unfamiliar situations where you lack knowledge. Don't let this intimidate you...take the opportunity to learn what your questions are - then do research before you make your spending decision. Soon you will feel confident with previously unfamiliar buying situations.

- Streamline your Shopping Trips - If you are too busy to avoid being a Passive Buyer, save more time by planning trips and combining them. Unplanned trips take longer because you don't know what you are going to get. Combining trips saves lots of time in the car as compared to separate trips. Again, if you place a value on your time you can be profitable by avoiding Passive Buying (or you can at least minimize the cost on your time).

Spending Personality IV - Avoidance Shopping

We've all heard the phrase "When the going gets tough, the tough get going". This is a good description of Avoidance Shopping. Avoidance Shoppers seek a way to escape the stress and pressure of life - shopping helps them "avoid reality" much like alcohol or drugs do for others. Unfortunately, this spending personality can cause a downward spiral where the pressures of life increase due to excessive and unnecessary spending.

Though you may not typically be an avoidance shopper, most of us at times exhibit these tendencies. We face a conflict or problem, and instead of dealing with it we avoid it. How many of us have ever had a bad day at work, or a fight with a loved one and gone shopping to "clear our heads"? Obviously, when shopping in such an emotional state, it is difficult to be rational and spend smart. Unfortunately as well, if this avoidance behavior becomes a habit, the original problem doesn't go away - it only festers and gets worse.

For some, Avoidance Shopping can be a result of needing to control others. A dominant personality may feel they need to exert their power if their dominance is threatened. Making a purchase that someone else doesn't agree with can be a way of demonstrating dominance. For others, avoidance shopping may be a way of getting even. Emotionally neglected spouses may buy items to get back at the person neglecting them. Again, Avoidance Shopping is a type of behavior which neglects the real issue.

How can you control Avoidance Buying?

- Be honest with yourself - admit to the real problem. The root of the spending personality is avoiding something unpleasant - hence it can be naturally difficult to recognize the behavior because it forces you to confront the problem (the very thing an Avoidance Shopper didn't want to do in the first place). Learn to be brutally honest with yourself when shopping - ask yourself "why am I really buying this"?

- Face up to the Underlying Problem or Issue - until you deal with the problem, it won't go away. Difficult as it may be, not dealing with the problem will possibly cause other problems in your life in addition to Avoidance Buying. For many, just becoming aware of the problem and facing it can provide resolution. If not, seek help from a trusted friend, clergy person or a professional counselor. Avoidance Buying is not necessarily the worst spending personality, but it can indicate a potential for much bigger emotional problems.

- Replace emotion with logic in spending. This course provides you with useful tools for doing this. Again, when you plan spending and can objectively analyze it, any impact of spending personalities are increased.

Overall, the best antidote to Avoidance Buying is to build healthy methods for coping with stress and problems. Many find that exercise is a great stress reducer because of the physical outlet it provides. Some find some area where they hope to improve themselves as excellent stress reducers. For example, if you want to learn to play the piano, a good time to practice is when stress flares up - this is a WIN/WIN situation - you allow the stress to subside while working on improving yourself.

Spending Personality V - Esteem Buying

Esteem Buying is the second most common spending personality after Impulse Buying. It is common among those most influenced by their peers (teens, social climbers, etc.). Esteem buying definitely makes the buyer feel good, but it can become a vicious cycle because of changing fads and tastes. In out materialistic society, possessions help people feel "they belong" or function as displays of success.

As part of a civilized society, we are taught to imitate the behavior of those we admire. The only problem is this socialistic tendency can create financial problems when we can't afford the prices our idols pay. "Keeping up with the Jones'" is one of the major contributing factors in exploding consumer debt. Advertising has done much to inflate the problem. Can't afford the status symbol you desire this month? No problem - CHARGE IT - EASY MONTHLY PAYMENTS!

How can you control Esteem Buying?

- Analyze the Reasons for Wanting Something - Be Honest! Could something less expensive (including something you already have) fill the need? Is the need real or imagined?

- Gain self-esteem in other ways - We all have a genuine need for self-esteem - there's nothing wrong with this - just find more productive, long-term methods for getting it. One of the best means of increasing self-esteem is to help someone else - especially those less fortunate than yourself. There is no way you can not feel better about yourself if you take an hour a month, or even a few times a year, to volunteer at a soup kitchen, visit residents at a nursing home or even just lend a supportive ear to a friend who is experiencing troubles.

- Recognize what True self-esteem is - it comes from being in control of life and having value as a person. Gain control by not allowing the fickle winds of trends to influence your purchase decisions - you will feel better about yourself by being true to what you value (spending smart!). You can gain value as a person by working on your relationships rather than spending money on them. Many parents purchase trendy items for their children as a way of trying to make up for time they don't spend with their children. Find the time instead (one way is to better plan your shopping trips?) - you'll save money, feel better about yourself and have better relationships.

Spending Personality VI - Overdone Buying

Overdone buying is typically related to a hobby or behavior. The problem of this personality arises when one becomes infatuated with a habit or hobby to the point where it causes financial problems. I'm sure we all know at least one Overdone Buyer who has become obsessed with the current Beanie Baby fad. Imelda Marcos' shoe collection is another recent good example.

Overdone Buying can also include the classic dependencies such as drugs, alcohol, eating, gambling, etc. These cause a double whammy as they can not only ruin your financial situation but can cause terrible health problems as well. For many, Overdone Buying begins as a simple method of avoiding behavior that gets out of hand. It can also result from attempts to compensate from something one feels is missing from their lives.

Some Overdone Behaviors can be good. Jack Nicklaus used to practice hitting 1000 golf balls a day. Thomas Edison spent every dime and minute he had trying to invent the electric light. You must determine whether an overdone behavior is good or bad. The question "Does the behavior help or hurt others or yourself" is the best measuring stick.

How can you control Overdone Buying?

- Recognize the Problem - as with all of the spending personalities, but especially overdone buying, you must recognize the problem before you can do something about it. A good warning sign is if the largest part of your disposable income (money after your bills) goes towards your behavior or hobby. Look objectively at others - is it "normal" to spend the amount of time and money on the behavior in question? Have you ever delayed paying bills in order to have more money for your habit?

- Avoid Situations that encourage the Behavior. Recovering alcoholics avoid bars, antique collectors avoid antique stores. Determine locations that trigger the habit and avoid them!

- Find a positive, healthy substitute - if something has been obsessively filling your life, there will be a void to be filled when you eliminate it. Find something else to do that provides a positive outlet while also not spending money unnecessarily.

Spending Personality VII - Hot Potato Buying

Hot Potato buying is a two-phase process of extremes. It typically begins with an extended period of consideration, with worried indecision, followed by impulsive action. The impulsive action phase is very similar to Passive buying. Hot Potato Buying usually occurs with a major purchase or financial decision and is often preceded by an emotional event. A good example would be when a spouse or relative dies and the survivors must decide what to do about investing the estate proceeds. The financial magnitude of the decision involved can make Hot Potato Buying one of the most dangerous spending personalities, even though the circumstances happen fairly rarely.

How can you control Hot Potato Buying?

- Let go of the Potato - If a traumatic or emotional event caused you to be in the position where a decision needs to be made, put it off for at least several months. If some purchase decision is causing you a great deal of worry, this is a sign to wait

- Educate yourself - If you are worried about a decision, take the time collect more information - when you educate yourself you will eventually feel absolutely confident in proceeding - there will be no more obsessive worry.

Psychology of Buying Summary

Most buying decisions are made on the basis of emotion. Emotions tend to be unpredictable and erratic for many of us. They are influenced by external events, by the things that happen to us. We need to change the buying decision process so it is based on logic.

Logic is predictable and stable. One of the most important aspects to Spend Smart success is being consistent. It doesn't matter so much how many Spend Smart ideas you use – what's more important is how consistently you use the ideas.

By understanding the Psychology of Buying, Spending Personalities and they process that happens when you make purchases, you have the opportunity to bypass emotion and move to a logical decision-making process. With a foundation of logic, or common sense, Spend Smart will reach it's greatest level of impact for you.

CHAPTER SIX
Seize Your Savings!

Having read a good part of this book, you are well on your way to becoming a Spend Smart graduate! You've set goals so you have your motivation – you know why you want to Spend Smart. You've learned the true Value of a Dollar, so you know why the dollars you hang on to, the dollars you save, are the most valuable dollars you'll ever have – much more valuable than dollars you earn. You've learned many Spend Smart Strategies and developed a Reverse Budget so you know how you are going to save money on your spending without making radical changes in your lifestyle. What's next?

Everything you've learned to date will help you save as much money as possible. However, saving money alone will not guarantee that you will end up with more money than month (instead of more month than money). You need to learn how to turn Spend Smart savings into money in your pocket. You need to learn how to SEIZE YOUR SAVINGS.

THE ONLY WAY TO TURN SPEND SMART INTO CASH IS TO SEIZE YOUR SAVINGS!

This book gives you many good ideas, tools and strategies. While having this information, learning how to save money on spending is important there is one vital component that must be added to make you successful. You must take action! This action will be your assurance that Spend Smart means real money in your pocket.

WITHOUT ACTION, SPEND SMART IS JUST ANOTHER GOOD IDEA.

You've had many good ideas in the past about saving money, haven't you? How much money have they actually put in your pocket? It's not just ideas that will get you ahead – it takes action as well. The action you need to take is to Seize your Savings! What do we mean by Seizing your Savings? Let's start by explaining what typically happens when someone saves money on spending. This will describe the situation you want to avoid.

Picture this if you will. A typical American consumer is at the mall shopping for some jeans. They find the perfect pair at one of their favorite stores. Since they have some time to kill, they decide to go look at another store before buying the jeans. At the second store, they find the jeans on sale for ten dollars less. What a deal! They buy the jeans and happily save ten dollars!

So now that they used Spend Smart and saved ten dollars, at the end of the month, they'll look in their pocket and they'll find an extra ten bucks, right? Probably not. What do you think will really happen?

This consumer will leave the store, pleased with their savings. Perhaps they will celebrate their good fortune by having lunch at the mall. They hadn't planned on this, but now they've got extra money. So they have lunch for five bucks. Then they decide to take a quart of that yummy frozen yogurt home as well! Even if they don't spend the ten bucks they saved that day at the mall, will the ten bucks still be in their wallet at the end of the month? Of course not…it will leak out of their pocket into some other spending, won't it?

So, if these people saved ten bucks on the jeans, but they don't have that ten bucks to claim as their own later, did these people save money? Well yes, but from a financial point of view did it really do them any good? Though they did use Spend Smart they also fell victim to impulse buying. This is typical of what happens to people when they save money on spending. When most people save money on something, they treat the money as "found" money, like if you found a twenty on the street. They tend to spend the savings on something else. When someone feels they have "extra money" they often make spending decisions the might not make otherwise.

Why does this happen? You probably know the feeling from personal experience. Hey, I saved some money – now I can do anything I want with it. There is an amazing phenomenon that seems to happen for most of us with money. Though we can't spend more than we have (forget about credit cards for a moment) we seem to be compelled to spend as much as we have. Another way to describe this is:

SPEND SMART RULE OF FINANCES – SPENDING INCREASES OR DECREASES AS AVAILABLE INCOME INCREASES OR DECREASES!

Now of course, you already knew that, didn't you? Think about it for a minute however – over the years what happens as you make more money? You spend more money! What do most people do when they have extra money? Do they save it or spend it? As we teach in Spend Smart, your financial success is much more dependent on spending than on income. Think of what happens when we get a raise or an income tax refund or our income increases in some way. Our first instinct is to spend it. We suddenly feel like we have all this extra money burning a hole in our pocket. We must do something with it!

Seizing your Savings is what you must do with your Spend Smart Savings. Seizing your Savings is what will turn the savings into dollars in your pocket, wallet or purse. Seizing your Savings is really a simple concept – in fact, many people already do something similar. Think about what happens with a 401K or any type of automated savings plan. The key to Seizing your Savings is to automate the process.

Think of how a 401K works. You want to put a portion of each paycheck into a savings plan. Maybe your take home pay would normally be $500 per week. You have decided to put $50 per paycheck into your 401K savings plan. For most of us with a 401K plan, this paycheck deduction happens automatically.

Each week you end up with $450 take home dollars instead of $500. $50 dollars is automatically going into your savings plan. For those of you that have an automatic payroll deduction, do you really miss that $50? Of course not – your spending changes to fit your available income. After a few months, you don't even notice it's gone.

Further, now that the $50 has been removed from your paycheck, what are the chances you will be able to spend it? If you are putting the $50 into a 401K, IRA or some other account where you get a tax deduction, you probably won't spend it just because of the penalties and taxes you'll be hit with (50% or more on a 401K or IRA) if you withdraw money before retirement. Doesn't this sound like a good way to make sure you save money? Make sure that the pain of spending it exceeds the pleasure of spending it!

Even if you don't put this money into a tax-qualified savings plan, if you simply got the $50 money out of your spend-able income, doesn't this increase the chances that it won't be spent? Our objective is to teach you how to make sure you have an extra $200 or $300 or more in your pocket at the end of each month.

THE WAY TO END UP WITH EXTRA MONEY EACH MONTH IS TO GET IT OUT OF YOUR POCKET/PURSE/WALLET!

Out of sight, out of mind is the concept behind Seizing your Savings. If you "hide" some money so it's not in your wallet or your checking account, that makes it more difficult to spend that money. If you don't have the money available to spend – **YOU WILL SPEND MUCH LESS!**

The millionaires in the *Millionaire Next Door* use a concept called "false scarcity" to make sure they have money left over for savings each month. With false scarcity, they run their households, they spend money, as if they had less money than they actually do. One good example of the way some people put false scarcity to use is when they get a raise, they continue to live as if they still had the same income and put all extra money from the raise into savings.

So how does this apply to Spend Smart? In order to end up with extra money each month, you must Seize your Savings…

YOU MUST TAKE THE MONEY YOU SAVE WITH SPEND SMART AND PUT IT SOMEPLACE WHERE YOU WON'T SPEND IT!

To Seize your Savings, you must create your own "personal 401K". To maximize the money you have left over at the end of the month, you must take a little from each paycheck and set it aside. To make sure you can live on less spend-able income, you must use your Reverse Budget and follow the Spend Smart Strategies you have chosen.

This is why your Reverse Budget is so important. You must feel absolutely comfortable with the Spend Smart Strategies you choose. You must be comfortable with the amount of money it will save you each month. Then once you are comfortable that by following these strategies, you will actually save this amount, you need to Seize your Savings and take the money you will save each month out of your spend-able income. Here's the process for Seizing your Savings each month:

	PROCESS	**DESCRIPTION**
1.	Review Your Reverse Budget	Make Sure You are Comfortable that you Can Do It!
2.	Figure Out What Your Savings Will be	Calculate a monthly total
3.	Seize your Savings	Take Money from Each Paycheck and "Hide" it

Let's review these steps.

First you must work on your Reverse Budget. You need to polish it and really refine it because you will use it to base your savings. You need to feel confident that you really will save this money because you are going to seize your savings and remove it from your paycheck or checking account. Make sure you have a Reverse Budget you feel good about.

Second, go over all your Spend Smart Strategies on your Reverse Budget and calculate what the savings will be. Some of your savings may be yearly figures, so you will need to convert these to monthly amounts. Estimate the items where you don't know what the exact monthly savings will be. It's

OK to be conservative – remember, any small savings you seize will be worth much more than large savings that don't end up in your pocket.

Finally, you need to Seize your Savings. Each paycheck, you need to take Spend Smart Savings out of it and put it someplace where you won't spend it. We'll talk in a minute about how you can actually take your savings from your paycheck and where you might consider hiding it.

You need to figure out how much you are going to take from each paycheck for Spend Smart savings. If you are paid twice a month, and your Reverse Budget says you are going to save $250 each month with Spend Smart, you need to seize $125 from each paycheck. If you are paid every two weeks, you need to take a little less than half of your monthly Spend Smart savings from each check. If you are paid weekly, you need to take a little more than on quarter of your monthly Spend Smart savings from each paycheck.

Here's a table to help you calculate exactly how much Spend Smart savings to seize from each paycheck:

If You Are Paid…	Seize This Amount of Savings
Every Week	23% of your Monthly Spend Smart Savings
Every 2 Weeks	46% of your Monthly Spend Smart Savings
Twice a Month	50% of your Monthly Spend Smart Savings
Monthly	100% of your Monthly Spend Smart Savings

Now of course, these amounts might vary a little depending on what bills you have due at certain times of month. Make no mistake about it however:

YOU MUST SEIZE YOUR SAVINGS FROM EACH PAYCHECK TO ACHIEVE YOUR SPEND SMART SUCCESS

Even if most of a given paycheck is "already accounted" for, for example, most of your first paycheck per month goes to the mortgage, you must still seize some Spend Smart Savings so it becomes a habit. Once Seizing your Savings becomes a habit, your success is insured. Make a commitment to false scarcity and begin acting like the financially successful people – start acting like a millionaire!

Let's review the Seize your Savings concept. First, you must calculate how much money you will save on spending each month by using Spend Smart. You begin using these strategies and start saving money. You need to Seize your Savings and remove your Spend Smart Savings from your spendable income. This will help you make sure you don't spend you savings and end up with no extra money at the end of the month. How can you remove money from your spend-able income in a way that is comfortable for you?

Remember, the more difficult you make it for you to spend your savings, the more likely you will actually begin to get ahead financially. We suggest a stair-step approach. This approach starts out with a plan where your Spend Smart savings are easy to get at in times of emergency. It progresses to levels where it is increasingly automated and more difficult to spend your savings.

The easiest and most comfortable way for people to begin Seizing their Savings is to use what we call the "Mattress" method. With the mattress method, you simply take the right amount of Spend Smart savings from each paycheck and put it under your mattress (or someplace else in your house).

Remember, since it is "out of sight" it is less likely that you will spend it. You know you will end up with enough money to pay your bills because you are using your Spend Smart strategies and your Reverse budget to save on spending. Seizing your Savings is simply a matter of removing these savings from your spend-able income. If you are concerned about not having enough money for unforeseen expenses, you can easily get at your growing pile of Spend Smart savings.

Try the mattress approach for a month or so. After a couple of months, when you have pile of several hundred dollars or more, you will get excited. You will become motivated to advance to the next step of Seizing your Savings.

With the next step, you want to get your savings further away from your spend-able income. With Step two of Seizing your Savings, you need to open a Spend Smart Savings account at your bank. Make sure you get a no-fee account! Now, each time you deposit or cash your paycheck, instead of putting the proper amount of cash under your mattress, deposit the money in your Spend Smart Savings account.

Make sure you can't write checks or get a debit card on this account. You want to make it more difficult to get at your savings. The best way to do this is to make sure you have to go to the bank to make a withdrawal. The money is still accessible if you should have an emergency, it's just a little more difficult to get at. That means you are less likely to spend it on an impulse item than if it you don't Seize your Savings or if you put your savings under your mattress.

Watch that bank balance grow for a couple of months, and you'll be ready to move to the next level of Seizing your Savings. In the third level, you automate the process of Seizing your Savings. Most banks allow you to automate regular transactions. For example, you can have your bank automatically pay certain bills, perhaps insurance payments, etc. each month. Why not have your bank automatically seize your savings!

Instead of making a deposit to your Spend Smart Savings account each time you get paid, have it done automatically! You can give your bank instructions to automatically transfer money from your checking account to your Spend Smart Savings account on any dates you choose. That way, you no longer have to make an effort to Seize your Savings.

For example, if you are saving $200 a month with Spend Smart, and have been making a $100 deposit into your Spend Smart Savings account every two weeks when you deposit your check, just ask your bank to automatically make this transfer for you. Tell them to transfer $100 from your checking to your Spend Smart Savings account a few days after you are paid. If you are paid on the 15th and 30th, ask them to make this transfer on the 17th and 1st of each month. Deposit your entire check and the bank will automatically Seize your Savings for you!

By automating this function, you greatly increase your chance for success. If you are making the deposit yourself each time you get paid, it can be easy for over confidence to set in. You might tell yourself, "Oh, I don't need to Seize my Savings this check, I know I won't spend it". No sooner than you say that, than you'll be walking through the mall, see a new stereo, and decide that "you deserve it"!

ONCE YOU BEGIN SEIZING YOUR SAVINGS, YOU MUST CONTINUE OR YOU WILL FEEL LIKE YOU HAVE EXTRA MONEY – AND EXTRA MONEY LEADS TO EXTRA SPENDING!

Having your bank make your Spend Smart deposits gets the Seize your Savings process to a level where your success becomes automatic. Not only are you following your Reverse Budget and saving money, that money is showing up as real cash in your savings account each month! That is control and power over your finances that most Americans never have. That is the power of Spend Smart.

The final level of Seizing your Savings is to further automate the process by having your employer make a direct deposit of your Spend Smart Savings to your Spend Smart Savings account each time they pay you. This is when Seizing your Savings becomes as automatic as a 401K plan. You are getting the money far away from your spend-able income because in order to access it, you must go to the bank and make a withdrawal. If you have an emergency, of course you can get at it. At the same time, the money is no longer as easy to spend, and it is automatically growing, each and every month.

Here is a summary of the different levels you should progress through as you are Seizing your Savings:

LEVEL	PROCESS	BENEFIT
1	Take Spend Smart Savings From Paycheck each Pay Period – Stuff it Under Your Mattress	Removes Money from (Immediately) Spend-able Income - Makes it More Likely Savings Will be There at the End of the Month
2	Open a Spend Smart Savings Account – Deposit Spend Smart Savings into Account Each Time you Cash/Deposit your Paycheck	Moves Spend Smart Savings Further From Spend-able Income – Make it More Difficult to Spend Savings
3	Have your Bank Automatically Transfer Spend Smart Savings from your Checking Account to you Spend Smart Savings Account	Automating the Process Increases the Likelihood that the Process Will Continue and you Will Continue to Seize your Savings
4	Have Your Employer Automatically Deposit Spend Smart Savings from your Paycheck to Your Spend Smart Savings Account	Out of Sight – Out of Mind – Just Like a 401K – Your Savings Continue to Grow – all you do is Follow your Reverse Budget!

Summary

You can be the best Spend Smart student ever, saving money on more spending than you ever though possible. Simply saving on spending however does not mean you will end up with a direct financial benefit. This doesn't mean Spend Smart will put extra money in your pocket. This doesn't mean you'll have extra money at the end of the month.

TO MAKE SURE SPEND SMART MEANS MONEY IN YOUR POCKET YOU MUST SEIZE YOUR SAVINGS!

You need to grab your savings, claim them, keep them for yourself before some store does! The best way to make sure you will see your Spend Smart savings as money in your pocket is to get it out of your spend-able income. In order to Seize your Savings, you must feel confident that you will actually save this money on your spending. You must be comfortable with the plan in your Reverse Budget. You must be confident that you can use the strategies and they will save you a specific amount of money.

Follow this plan for Seizing Your Savings. Start out at a level you feel comfortable with, perhaps the mattress approach or the savings account approach. We don't want anyone losing sleep worried they won't have enough money to pay their bills with. As you gain confidence over the months, you will feel comfortable enough to begin automating the process.

Think about how your growing pile of Spend Smart Savings will change your life. Do you have a six-month income cushion as we all know we should have? Are you confident that you can pay for emergencies that may come up? By Seizing your Savings, you are not only building towards your Spend Smart goals, you are building that income cushion that we all dream of.

No one else is as concerned about your financial situation and future than you are. You have done a great service to yourself by reading this book. We encourage you to continue your learning by reading other books or by attending classes such as Spend Smart and Debt Free & Prosperous Living. Remember however, knowledge alone won't make financial success happen. You must take action on what you learn.

As with all other Spend Smart concepts, you have to decide what makes sense for you. You need to figure out how to apply what you've learned to your specific situation. Start at a comfortable level and build from there. If you are uncomfortable with Seizing all your Savings immediately than start Seizing 2/3rds or ½. As your comfort grows, so too will your savings.

Your goal needs to be to get to the point where you automatically Seize your Savings. When you reach this level, your financial destiny will be changed forever. You will be on your way to becoming financially successful. If you've never been able to find money for investing before, you will now. If you want to begin paying off your debt and getting out of debt quickly you now will have the money to make it happen. If you simply want to build a six-month income cushion, it will now start growing for you.

Don't let everything you've learned go to waste. Seize Your Savings. Control your financial future by controlling your spending and reap the rewards. You know the line – **JUST DO IT!**

CHAPTER SEVEN
APPLIANCES

The biggest expense of any appliance is typically electric and/or gas costs. The electric usage estimates are based upon tables found in your workbook. The cost estimates are based on an the national average of 7900 kilowatt-hours used each year at an average rate of 9 cents per kilowatt-hour (*Source – Edison Electric Institute, Typical Bills, Summer 1997*). Refer to the conversion table in the appendix to calculate your savings if your electric cost is different than 9 cents per kilowatt-hour.

Air Conditioner

Average annual air conditioner use is around 1500 hours (of course it's more in the south and less in the north). A typical air conditioner uses 1 Kilowatt of electricity each hour. Average annual electric costs for an air conditioner are $135. Adjust this number up if you are in the southern US.

Install air conditioners on north or east facing windows - south and west-facing windows receive more sun and make the unit work harder.

Choosing an energy-saving central air conditioner instead of a standard model saves up to 35 percent each hour you run your unit. **Save $47 per year.**

Many electric companies offer a Central Air Conditioner Rebates program which gives you money back for buying an energy-saving model. Rebates range up to $300 for qualifying units purchased on or after May 1, 1996. Ask your central air conditioner dealer or electric company for details.

Dishwasher

Approximate Average Water Costs:

Cold water - ¼ cent per gallon
Hot Water - 1 ¼ cent per gallon
(includes water and heating costs)

With most dishwashers, you don't need to waste water and time by washing dishes off with running water in the sink - simply scrape off food, then put the dishes in the dishwasher - Each time you wash dishes you can save 30 gallons. **Save $26/yr on cold water, $135/yr hot.**

If you feel you must rinse dishes first - fill up the sink instead - you still save 25 gallons of water. **Save $22/yr on cold water, $113/yr hot.**

Use the short/light wash cycle - save electricity by using 25% less hot water - try it and see how your dishes come out - they should be fine (especially if you pre-rinse in the sink). **Save $13/yr with gas water heater - $34/yr with electric water heater.**

Dishwasher energy use (with 140-degree hot water) is $136/year for electric water heater and $53/year for gas water heaters.

Turn hot water heater down from 140 degrees to 120 degrees - try your dishwasher and see how it works at the lower temperature. With newer models, it should be fine. **Save $24 to $45/yr.**

Air dry your dishes in the dishwasher - most models allow you to punch a button for air dry - Crack the door after the last rinse cycle. **Save $12 to $23 a year.**

Refrigerator/Freezer

Refrigerators are the appliances that use the most electricity - up to 8% of your electric bill or 16% of you electric bill if you heat with gas. This is $85 to $283 per year.

Do you have an extra refrigerator in the garage or basement for keeping drinks, etc. cold? If it's older than a 1993 model it costs you $150 to $283 per year in electricity to keep your drinks cold! Post-1993 models still cost $60 to $108 per year to cool your pop.

If your refrigerator is pre-1993, consider getting a new, more efficient one - it will pay for itself in electricity savings in about 5 years. **Save $90 to $223 per year.**

Set refrigerator temperature controls in the mid range (38 F to 42 F). Each degree you raise the refrigerator temperature = 2.5% decrease in electricity use. If you can raise the temperature 4 degrees this is a 10% electricity savings. **Save $6 to $28 dollars per year.**

Side-by-side units use 35% more energy in the post 1993 units - 50% more energy in the pre-1993 units. Next time you buy a refrigerator, get an upright unit. **Save $21 to $38 per year.**

Clean your refrigerator's condenser coils (underneath or on the back) several times a year. (If you have a longhaired pet, you may need to do this more often.) Use a soft bristle attachment on your vacuum - increase efficiency and life of refrigerator.

Check the seal to make sure it's clean and tight. To test for tightness, close the door on a piece of paper and try to pull it out. Test along the length of the gasket - wipe the gasket often with warm water to prolong life.

Don't keep the refrigerator by heat sources like stoves, dishwashers, direct sunlight - causes more energy use.

Turn on the power-saver (condensation or energy-switch) unless you see moisture forming on the outside of the refrigerator.

Cover all containers so the refrigerator doesn't have to work as hard to control humidity.

When buying a freezer, avoid a used model because they are less energy-efficient. The initial price might be low, but you'll more than make up the difference with higher electric bills each month you use the freezer.

Chest Freezers use 10 to 15% less energy than uprights - because they are better insulated and the heavy cold air does not flow out when the door is opened. Get a chest freezer and **save $6 to $12 (post-1993) or $25 to $45 per year (pre-1993).**

Auto-defrost freezers use about 40% more energy than manual-defrost models - manual freezers should be defrosted when they have ¼ inch of ice. Forget the auto-defrost and **save $16 to $31 per year (post 1993) or $30 to $65 per year (pre-1993).**

Defrost the freezer when ice builds up to 1/4 inch thick. **Save $5 to $19 a year.**

Set freezer thermostat controls so the freezer temperature is about 0 F (the point where ice cream is hard, but still "scoop-able".

Freezers packed with food are more efficient than nearly empty ones. Keep it at least 2/3 full. Freeze jugs of water to help retain cold temperature when the freezer is less full.

Get rid of old freezers that aren't kept full. Depending on the type of freezer you have, **save $60 to $155 each year.**

Stoves/Oven

Use the smallest cooking appliance to get the job done. For example, microwave ovens, toaster ovens, crock pots and electric skillets use less electricity than ranges or ovens.

Preheat your oven only for baking. Otherwise, put the dish in when you turn the oven on. If you use your oven 4 times per week, **save $12 per year.**

Turn off the oven 30 minutes before the dish is done - the trapped heat will finish the job. If you use your oven 4 times per week, **save $43 per year.**

Don't peek! Every time you open the oven door you lose ¼ of the heat.

Put a nail through a baking potato to reduce cooking time by 15 minutes.

Turn on the self-cleaning function while the oven is still hot from baking.

Use a lid and a lower setting on your electric range - still gets the cooking done, just a little slower. **Save $19 per year.**

Use the smallest pan possible and match the burner size to the pan. Doubling the burner size doubles the electricity use.

Cooking with a lid on decreases cooking time and energy use by 20%. If you use the stove top 5 hours per week, **save $14 per year.**

Once water boils, turn the heat to low - a slow boil is as hot as a rolling boil.

Cooking on stovetop burners is inefficient because heat dissipates into the air. Use the microwave whenever possible. Using the microwave half the time instead of the stovetop, **save $26 per year.**

Microwaves use 2 to 3 times less energy than an oven - use the microwave whenever possible - try baking potatoes in them!

Get at least a 600-watt microwave - most microwaves are used for simple tasks (re-heating, cooking vegetables, warming coffee, etc.) - You probably don't need the bells and whistles of high-end units.

The FDA recommends a way to test your dishes for microwave use - microwave the container for 1 minute - if it is warm or hot - don't use it - if it is lukewarm - use for re-heating - if it is still cool - use for cooking.

Cover dishes when using the microwave - this will speed cooking time.

Washer/Dryer

Automatic shut-off on dryers save money - WHY? – They save money because most people set extra time on the dryer to make sure the clothes get dry.

Use cold water washing with cold rinse whenever possible - it will clean all but the filthiest of clothes - if you have hard water - warm wash/cold rinse will work well. If you wash just five loads of laundry per week, cold water washing **saves $67 per year** - warm water washing **saves $44 per year.**

General

When buying gas appliances (dryer or oven) get one with electronic ignition instead of pilot light models which use 30% more gas - **save $30 per year.**

Coffee Makers use a huge amount of electricity. Limit the hours the coffee maker is on and be sure it's off when you leave home. Turn it off after brewing coffee, and use the microwave to reheat coffee instead of leaving the pot on all day or keep the fresh coffee in a thermos. For each hour per day that you keep the coffee maker off, **save $37 per year.**

Extended Warranties - are they worth it? - NO - This is insurance - insurance is a losing gamble because the company must make money (odds are stacked against you). Insurance to protect against a major disaster makes sense - insurance to protect against minor mishaps doesn't make sense - appliance problems are not major disasters. Warranties pay out 10 to 15 cents for every dollar taken in premium. Buy appliances with good reliability records.

Used appliances may not be your best option because new appliances have much better energy efficiency.

Home appliance repair - you can get appliance repair instructions free from the manufacturers over the phone - GE (Hotpoint and RCA) 800-626-2000 - Whirlpool (Roper, Kitchenaid) 800-253-1301 - RCA electronics 800-336-1900 - Maytag 800-688-9900 - Amana - 800-843-0304. If you save just one visit from the appliance repairperson per year **save $70 per year**.

Clean VCRs/Camcorders with Scotch cleaning tape - it isn't abrasive and won't wear down your heads like other cleaning tapes.

VCRs/Camcorders cleaning - most repair people say you should clean them at least once a year. The length of time isn't as important as the amount of usage. To extend VCR/Camcorder life, typically, you should get them professionally cleaned every 600 to 700 hours of use. If you use the VCR/Camcorder once or twice a week this is probably about every three years.

Wear the neck strap when using a camera/camcorder - dropping these devices is the most common cause for repair.

Water heater - drain about a gallon from the faucet valve twice per year (once if you have soft water) - prolongs water heater life and allows more efficient heating.

CHAPTER EIGHT
AUTOMOBILES

Automobile costs are our second largest lifetime expense. Many times, we don't stop and consider that there are more to automobile costs than just gas. After the purchase, one of the biggest expenses is auto insurance. We'll talk about that more in another chapter. Let's look at the ownership costs and the operating costs of typical automobiles.

Car Costs (*Source - Runzheimer International*)

- Ownership Costs including taxes, depreciation, finance charges, registration, insurance and license fees (based on 4 year, 60,000 miles) - these costs are fixed whether you drive the car or not:

Automobile Ownership Costs			
	Compact 4 cylinder	Sedan 6 cylinder	Luxury 8 cylinder
Per Mile	8.3 cents	10.0 cents	11.2 cents
Ownership Cost	$11.92/day	$13.60/day	$15.51/day

Your car costs you money even if you don't drive it!

The best way to save money on ownership costs is to buy the right kind of vehicle in the right way to begin with.

The Right Kind of Car

In almost all cases, if you want to get the best car value, if you want to Spend Smart, buy a late model (2 to 3 years old) used car. Why do we say this? Depreciation is the largest cost of owning a new car. New cars lose up to 50% of their value in depreciation the first two or three years. Used cars also cost less than new cars to insure.

Buy a "like new" used car and **Save thousands of dollars**

Hear are some tips about buying a used car:

- Buy cars that have consistent records of 100,000+ miles with little maintenance or problems - check Consumer Reports and www.autobytel.com or www.edmunds.com on the web.

- Since you'll probably be selling your car some day, small and medium-sized sedans are often the best buy - performance cars give their best in their early years - luxury cars retain their value.

- Old cars with low mileage often are the best buys - age of the vehicle is viewed as a major component of price - but mileage is the "true age" of a car. A four year-old car with 20,000 miles is probably a better value than a two year-old car with 40,000 miles.

- Prices fluctuate with season - November, December, January are usually the best time to buy a car because buyers are scarce – they're spending all their money on Christmas/Hanukah!

- Someone selling their own car can offer the best deals because they don't need a markup - a dealer will want the retail price or close to it - a private party is more likely to sell at or below wholesale Blue Book value.

- Disadvantage of buying from a private party is you don't get a warranty - though you might be able to negotiate a short one - maybe one month.

- When choosing a used car, call around and ask auto mechanics about their experience with frequency of repairs and types of repairs for year, make and model you are considering.

- Make sure you have a trusted mechanic check out a car before you buy it.

- Try to contact the previous owner of the car if you buy through a dealer - they can talk honestly about it's shortcomings - In most states, the dealer must by law, disclose this information.
- Never buy a used car without seeing the ownership documents - make sure the Vehicle Identification Number (VIN) on the driver's side of the dashboard matches the VIN on the title and registration.

- Check out www.carfax.com on the web – you can purchase a complete title history including whether the car has been totaled, had flood damage, been stolen, had odometer tampered with, etc. For $19 it is worth the peace of mind to get this information before you buy. All you need is the VIN.

- Friends can be a good source for vehicles because you trust each other - of course, if problems arise, your friendship may suffer.

- If a car is still under warranty, check the owners manual and see if it can be transferred.

The Right Way to Buy a Car

What's the right way to buy a car? Let's start with the wrong way. If you want to Spend Smart, the wrong way to buy a car is to lease it! Of course, leasing isn't "buying" so really we should title this section *The Right Way to Pay for a Car*.

If your goal is to keep automobile costs down, buying is much better than leasing a car. The three largest costs in automobile ownership are depreciation, insurance and finance charges. Leasing tends to maximize all of these costs.

When leasing a car:

- Depreciation is maximized because you generally only have the car two or three years – this is the period when the car loses the greatest portion of it's value. Of course, someone has to pay this depreciation cost – who pays it? – that's right, you do!

- Insurance costs are maximized because leases typically require you to have a low deductible. Of course, low deductible insurance policies require the highest insurance premiums.

- Interest charges are typically higher than with a car loan.

There is only one reason why most people consider a lease. That is because they are focused on the monthly payment instead of the total cost of transportation. It's true that you can get "more" car for a lower payment with a lease as compared to buying a car. With a lease however, your payments never end (unless you give up the car). With a purchase, eventually your payments will stop.

A good analogy comparing leasing to buying is comparing an interest-only loan to a regular loan. Your payments on the interest-only loan are smaller, but you never pay off the debt. Your payments on the regular loan are higher, but eventually you own the car free and clear.

Don't lease a car. If you can't afford the payment on the car you want, downsize what you want.

THE BEST WAY TO BUY A CAR IS TO PAY CASH!

That probably sounds impossible to do, but suspend your disbelief for a moment. You would agree that the lowest cost way to buy a car is to buy a used car with cash, wouldn't you. You don't lose piles of money to depreciation, your insurance rates are lower and your finance costs are zero.

One of our goals with Spend Smart is to help you build a pile of money. Money that you can choose to use as you like. Many people like the idea of owning a car instead of just making payments. My favorite kind of car is one that is paid for!

Maybe you will set a goal to buy your next car with cash. That was a goal for my wife and I. Two years ago, our financial life was a disaster. We never had any extra money left over at the end of the month. We began to follow the Spend Smart way. Recently, we purchased a 2 year-old, like-new mini-van. We were able to pay for it with cash. You can do it to if you apply what you learn in Spend Smart.

Let's look at the second type of automobile expenses, operating costs. Operating cost include gas, oil, maintenance and tires. Here's a chart showing typical operating costs:

Average Cost per Mile Including Operating and Ownership Costs			
	Compact 4 cylinder	Sedan 6 cylinder	Luxury 8 cylinder
10,000 miles / year	43.1 cents	50.4 cents	63.2 cents
15,000 miles / year	37.3 cents	43.1 cents	47.7 cents
20,000 miles / year	33.8 cents	38.6 cents	42.6 cents

Average annual gas cost per car at 25 MPG = $700 for gas - 13,000 miles

The best way to save on operational costs with your car is with regular, proper, maintenance done by you! Proper maintenance saves money on future repairs and saves money on gas costs today!

Fuel Economy

- Air conditioners eat 2.5 MPG ($70/year) - if you are going 40 mph or less, it is cheaper to have the windows open - if you are going more than 40 mph, the wind resistance of open windows uses more fuel than the air conditioner.

- AAA (American Automobile Association) says an out-of-tune car uses 3% to 8% more gasoline. Keep your engine in tune and **save $21 to $54 per year.**

- Think aerodynamically. Bike carriers, ski racks, those car-top storage bins that look like extra-large Big Mac boxes: All can interfere with your car's aerodynamic profile and cost you gas mileage. Remove racks, etc. when not in use and increase fuel efficiency as much as 10% - **save $70 per year.**

- How much Octane do you need? The 87 found in regular grade unleaded? The 89 found in super grade? The 91 found in premium grade? Advertising has convinced us to buy more octane than needed - most cars run fine on regular - try a lower grade with your car - if it pings/knocks - try a different gas station (quality varies) - if pinging continues, switch to a higher grade.

- According to AAA, less than 10% of the cars on the road today need premium-grade gasoline. Even so, about 20% of drivers buy it--and pay roughly 17 cents a gallon extra for the privilege. Cut out the premium gas and **save $88 per year**. Cut out super gas and **save $36 per year**.

Maintenance / Repairs

- Frequent Oil changes (every 3500 miles) are the biggest contributor to a car going 250,000+ miles.

- Learn to change your own oil (check owners manual) - it's cheaper and faster than taking it someplace - approximate cost $10 - prices at shops range from $20 (with coupon) to $50 - average car need 5 changes per year - for each car, **save $50 to $150 per year.**

- Don't buy oil additives - save your money - when they are fresh, they are effective, however, they don't drain well during an oil change and build-up over time - proper oil changes are just as effective.

- Get a tune-up every 12 to 15,000 miles or every year - tune-ups are more than paid back in improved mileage and prolonged engine life.

- Prolong life of windshield wipers by sanding the edges.

- Starting problems are often related to corroded battery terminals - clean them occasionally with baking soda - coat them with a thin coat of petroleum jelly.

- When obvious problems arise (squeaking brakes, etc.), don't procrastinate getting them fixed - more than likely, waiting will cause additional damage and cost more to fix.

- Avoid car dealers for parts and service unless it is covered by warranty - they consistently charge 1 ½ to 2 times more than independent mechanics.

- Find a good quality, low-priced independent mechanic - ask your friends and neighbors - ask the local auto parts stores - you'll know one when you find it - reservations need to be made at least a week in advance.

- Get several quotes on major work.

- For brake jobs, mufflers or front-end alignment - go to a shop that specializes in these - again. Look for independents (not chains like Midas, etc. who have national advertising campaigns to support).

- Windshield ding? Nicks smaller than a quarter can be stopped from spreading - why do you care? Replacement can be $300 to $700 - even if your insurance covers it your rates will probably go up. First cover the nick on both sides with scotch tape. Go to a shop that repairs windshields and offers a one-year guarantee. Cost is under $100.

Rental Cars

- Auto Rental Discounts abound (AAA, AARP, frequent fliers, USAA, etc.) - determine whether your auto insurance or credit card covers you in rental car.

- When renting a car, rent from off-airport sites - typically save 30% (up to $100 on a one-week rental).

- Call 800 numbers of car rental companies to compare rates - rates vary from city to city, time of year - no company is the lowest all the time.

Tires

- Under-inflated tires increase fuel use by 2% for each missing pound of pressure according to AAA - if your tires are supposed to be at 30 PSI and they're at 25 PSI your losing 10% of your gas mileage. Keep your tires properly inflated at 30 PSI instead of 25 PSI - **save $70 per year.**

- Even if your tires hold pressure well, every 10-degree change in temperature changes pressure 1% - need extra air in winter, less air in summer. In the fall and winter when the temperature can decrease suddenly, you need to check your pressure often. If there's a 30 to 50 degree swing in a few days, the pressure will change.

- To check your tires, don't rely on the air pump at your local gas station; it may be way off. Instead, invest in your own tire pressure gauge (they're about the size of a fountain pen and usually cost under $3). Check your tires when they're "cold"—that is, haven't been driven for more than a mile.

- Rotate tires - every 5 to 10,000 miles - extends tire life - check your tire manual for proper rotation pattern. Easy to do. Take off one tire and put your spare on - rotate that tire to it's next position, etc. End with the final rotated tire replacing the spare and put the spare back in the trunk.

Some tire dealers will rotate and balance your tires for life when you purchase tires - if not, rotate tires yourself and **save $50 per year.**

- Bad alignment is the biggest killer of tires - some shops give you lifetime alignment service on your car when you pay for an alignment - saves gas too.

CHAPTER NINE
BABIES AND CHILDREN

Children are a wonderful blessing for parents. There is nothing that can compare to the joy of watching and helping a child grow up. Though there are plenty of heartbreaks as well, talk to most parents and they will tell you that despite the hardships, they wouldn't trade being a parent for anything.

Of course, there is a financial price to this joy. Recent studies have estimated the cost of providing for a child to age 18 is over $180,000. WOW! And you thought the total you pay for your house in mortgage payments was big!

Now I don't know about you, but I don't believe raising a child has to be that expensive. We have four children ourselves and know many couples with several kids. I can promise you, none of these families have the extra money to support as high a level of spending as the study suggests.

Raising children is without a doubt one of the toughest areas of Spend Smart to apply. As Spend Smart parents we are torn between the natural desire to give our kids everything they need, nothing but the best and the desire to live sane financial lives. Is there a happy medium between these two desires?

IN ORDER TO EFFECTIVELY SPEND SMART WITH REGARD TO YOUR CHILDREN, YOU MUST FOCUS ON THE BIG PICTURE, THE LONG TERM.

Yes, you feel at least a short-term satisfaction when you buy nice clothes for your kids, overwhelm them with more toys than can fit in their room or buy them a new bike every year for their birthday. In order to Spend Smart however, you must weigh that short-term satisfaction against the long-term consequences. Instead of looking at changing your spending on your children as a negative, consider the positive consequences.

With Spend Smart, you will achieve financial stability. With financial stability your life will have much less stress. Money worries won't dominate your home life. You can focus on developing your relationship with your children instead of paying for their next pair of $150 sneakers.

If you apply Spend Smart, in all areas of your life including your kids, you'll be able to spend time at night reading to your kids instead of worrying about the bills. You'll be able to be in a position where you can choose private schools for them if that's important to you. You can set a wonderful example of careful spending instead of wasteful and frivolous spending. Perhaps best of all from your child's perspective, you will be better able to provide for your own retirement and won't be dependent on them for support.

So decide what you want for your kids. Do you want to give them a healthy, stable home life or the latest expensive toy fad? Do you want to set an example for learning the important things in life or set an example of clawing out an income to pay for more and more materialistic stuff?

The most important thing to kids is getting attention and support from their parents, even if they throw a fit at Target because you won't buy them the latest Power Ranger. They need parents, not Santa Claus year-round. Your children's future is at stake. Spend Smart is the right thing to do.

Let's look at some Spend Smart ideas for babies and children. Why not start at the beginning?

Infant Accessories

The first big expense most parents are hit with are all the different item of baby "furniture" and accessories.

- Don't buy a bassinet. If you are given one, that's different, but why buy one when it will be used for such a short period of time - clothes baskets or a large drawer covered with a quilt work fine - or just use the crib from day one.

- Baby bathtubs – you already have one - your kitchen sink works fine with a towel lining it - use a clothesbasket and towel in the tub to keep baby from sliding around.

- Traveling crib? An inflatable wading pool serves an excellent double role.

- Consider a portable high chair that grips the table – they are less expensive and easy to travel with.

- It is smart to buy baby clothes one or two sizes too big because they grow too fast!

- Baby soaps are expensive and not needed - use a plain-Jane soap low in scents, additives and antibacterial additives – Ivory is terrific.

- Jars of baby food are convenient for occasional use, but expensive for everyday use - easy and economical to puree or mash the food you prepare for the rest of the family - you can puree large amounts in advance and freeze it in ice cube trays.

- Baby juice costs two to three times as regular juice - pediatricians say you can use regular juice and dilute it 50/50 with water - though the baby juice may have some additional vitamins, if you are feeding your child properly anyway, these vitamins are just overkill.

Most baby items (cribs, highchairs, swings, etc.) can be found inexpensively at garage sales, second-hand baby stores, etc. Look at chapter 19 entitled "Slightly Used" for some excellent ideas. Consider getting many clothes this way too - the baby doesn't know if the label says Gymboree or "GarageSaleboree". You can save hundreds of dollars here - the only thing stopping you is ego!

Young Children

The toughest Spend Smart challenge presented by young children, age 2 to 7 is that they can talk! They can tell you what they want you to buy for them. Not only that, they can whine, cry and throw tantrums in stores. Obviously, this can lead to the worst type of spending, impulse or unplanned spending.

The first thing you need to know about this challenge is that you are not alone! Even though we tend to think our children are perfect at times, when it comes to the "gimmees", it seems like no other children are as bad. Trust me, as a long-time observer of human nature, no matter how difficult it is to believe, your kids are no different than most others when it comes to wanting more stuff than you are willing to buy.

Now I don't claim to be an expert, but I can share some ideas from first hand experience of how to minimize the problems of the kids who want everything. Try them and see what works for you:

- Let your child be involved in the things you plan on buying for them. Whether it's clothes, school supplies or even grocery shopping, let kids have a say. Often times the issue of wanting things is a control issue. Children want to feel that they have a say, that their opinion counts.

- The best way to give children a say is to give them choices. You are able to control the range of their choices and they feel good about making a choice.

- Use lists when you shop. When a child wants something, explain to them that you can't get it because it's not on the list.

- Help your kids start a master list of things they want. When they demand you buy something for them in a store tell them they cannot have it now, but if it's really important to them they can add it to the list. Often just adding it to the list will satisfy their demand.

- Use the master list for Christmas / Birthday presents. Tell them they can pick a certain number of items they have on the list. This is excellent because it helps kids begin to understand that they often must make choices of what is most important to them

- If you travel on business, kids come to expect something when your return home. After buying expensive souvenirs for a while, I learned that they kids didn't care so much what they got, as long as they got something. Solution – I stop at the dollar store on the way home from the airport.

- Don't buy gifts at the airport for your kids – talk about highway (or is it runway) robbery!

- Learn to say no and mean it! (I'm not good at this one).

- Avoid the impulse buying in the first place. Plan on letting your child "get a treat" on a shopping trip, put it on your list and set ground rules in advance. Once you let a child get one impulse item, before your shopping trip is over they'll want more.

As with infants, kids go through certain types of items so quickly, buying everything new can be a huge waste of money. Spend Smart and consider gently used items. Again, chapter 19 is a great resource!

CHAPTER TEN
BANKING/MONEY/DEBT

The biggest problem most of us have with money is overconfidence. We assume we know pretty much everything we need to know. Some of you may have some initial resistance to Spend Smart. I mean, come on, we all know how to save money on spending, don't we?

Though we may already know a great deal about saving on spending, how many of us feel confident we know everything needed to achieve financial success? Spend Smart is all about financial success. It's not about saving a few bucks here and there – it's about changing our financial future by changing our spending. Though this chapter is not very long, the most important Spend Smart concept is contained here. Let's get it out front right now:

THE BIGGEST OBSTACLE STANDING BETWEEN YOU AND FINANCIAL SUCCESS IS DEBT!

Debt! How can debt be a problem? I mean, using credit is "smart money" isn't it? The only party for whom credit is smart money is the person making the loan, not the person taking the loan.

Think about this for a moment. We all know we need to invest money, a pretty good amount of money, to become financially secure. Since you are reading this book, I would bet you are not investing as much money you should be or would like to be. Am I right?

Did you know, for the typical American, their single largest expense is debt? We spend more money on debt – car loans, mortgages, credit cards, home equity loans, etc. than any other expense area.

IF YOU COULD ELIMINATE YOUR DEBT, THINK ABOUT HOW MUCH MONEY YOU WOULD HAVE TO INVEST!

Teaching you how to eliminate your debt is not the purpose of Spend Smart. Make no mistake about it however, you can completely wipe out your debt, faster than you would have ever believed possible and Spend Smart can help you do it!

Those of us who teach Spend Smart also teach a course known as *Debt Free & Prosperous Living™*. Based on what as *Debt Free & Prosperous Living™* teaches us, let us now give you the NUMBER ONE SPEND SMART STRATEGY:

BECOME DEBT FREE!

- Pay off all of your debt and REDUCE YOUR TOTAL MONTHLY EXPENSES BY 42%! Though this isn't the purpose of this class, Spend Smart ties in with our Debt Free & Prosperous Living class. We teach the typical American how to get completely out of debt in just 5 to 7 years, including their mortgage, using nothing more than the money they currently bring home.

We'll talk more about debt here in a minute. For the time being, just know that the quickest route to financial freedom is debt freedom. Spend Smart can help you achieve debt freedom. SO don't think of Spend Smart as just a way to help you save a couple of hundred bucks a month. If you learn how to eliminate your debt and your monthly payments…

SPEND SMART CAN HELP YOU SAVE $1000, $1500, $2500 OR MORE EACH AND EVERY MONTH!

Let's look at some specifics about Banking/Money/Debt

<u>BANKING/MONEY</u>

- According to Consumer Reports, the average person pays $164 per year in bank fees. Find out what the fees are for. With today's highly competitive banking market, many banks offer no-fee checking and no-fee savings – switch to a bank that doesn't charge fees and **save $164 per year!**

- Don't buy checks from the bank – you can get them much cheaper from commercial printing companies – Call Checks in the Mail - 800-733-4443 - Current Inc. - 800-426-0822 - Image Checks - 800-562-8768.

- If you come into some "found money" from, for example, a tax refund, inheritance or bonus, wait a while before you make any spending decisions. The longer you hold on to money, the more it will feel like your money.

- ATM fees can be a killer, especially if you use an ATM that is out of your bank's network. Most banks don't charge an ATM fee if you use one of their machines. Get a map or listing of where your bank's ATMs are – keep it in your car so you always can locate the nearest one. The typical ATM holder uses their card 6 times a month. If you only use your banks ATMs, you'll save at least $1.50 per use – **save $108 per year.**

CREDIT/DEBT

If you really want to Spend Smart in the area of credit and debt, ask your Spend Smart instructor when the next Debt Free & Prosperous Living class will be held. Prior to eliminating your debt however, there are some Spend Smart Strategies to reducing the amount of money you spend on and with debt.

- When using credit cards, ask yourself whether you'd pay the same price -- or even purchase the item at all -- if you were paying cash. Studies show people spend as much as 100% more when using a credit card.

- Pay off as much credit card debt as you feel comfortable doing with savings - you'll come out ahead by a large amount of interest - if you have emergency, you still have a credit card but it doesn't have a balance!

- If you can't pay off the credit card balances, pay more than the minimum - you get a much better return than most investments because it is an after-tax, guaranteed 17% (national credit card average) rate of return.

- If you can't pay off all of your credit card debt now, negotiate a lower rate with your card company. Call your credit card companies and tell them you have received an offer to transfer your balance to another card at a lower rate. Many 5.9% or lower introductory rates are now available for first 6 to 12 months. One note of caution, if you regularly transfer credit card balances to new lower-rate cards, this can be a negative on your credit report.

- Average total credit card balance is $7400 at 17% interest - if you can get it down to 10% the average person will **save $518 year!** - get it down to 5.9% and you'll save **$814 per year!**

- Want to really save some money? Accelerate your mortgage payoff - **save as much as $50,000 to $100,000 or more.**

- Debt consolidation loans? Be careful here. Debt consolidation loans typically decrease monthly payments. This can be dangerous because it makes people feel they have "more money". This seems good until you consider that decreased payments also mean you'll be making payments for a longer period of time. Don't consider a debt consolidation loan unless you enroll in an automated debt elimination program. Such a program uses the money you "save" on lower monthly payments to automatically elimination your debt. Ask your instructor or contact Premier Financial Solutions, Inc. for more information.

CHAPTER ELEVEN
CLOTHES/SHOES

Experts calculate the average family spends nearly 10% of income on clothing/shoes! Therefore it makes Spend Smart sense to try and reduce these expenses where possible. For many people, buying nice clothes helps them feel good about themselves. We certainly are in favor of positive self-esteem.

Remember however, Spend Smart is not about living like a hermit or drastically changing your lifestyle. Like many other areas of spending, it's simple a matter of making some choices where you increase the buying power of your dollar, avoid buying things you won't use often and extend the useful lifetime of your purchases. Don't stop buying nice clothes – just use Spend Smart Strategies!

- Extend the useful life of your clothes by buying classic styles - buy white shirts, blue blazer, etc - don't buy the latest fad because their popularity will fade and you won't have gotten maximum value from your purchase.

- A $50 dress that is worn often makes more sense than a $30 dress worn once.

- Experts say 1/3 of all clothing purchased is rarely worn because of poor choices in color, style and fit - a garment that is worn is a much better deal than one that sits in the closet. Don't buy clothing on impulse!

- The true cost of clothing is not just the price – it's the quality as well. Buying low-cost clothing that lacks in quality will not save you money in the long run. Carefully inspect items for durability or you'll be replacing them often. Check for tight stitching, double stitching, pockets that lay flat - avoid loose seams, seams that don't lay flat, poorly finished edges that will unravel.

- Buy men's suits with two pairs of pants - pants wear out much sooner than coats - if you can buy a suit for $200 and get an extra pair of pants for as much as $100 (they often need to be special ordered) it's like getting two suits for $300.

- Consider private label/store label clothing - the markup is 60% to 80%. Brand name items have a lower markup of 50% to 60%.

- Private label items will be on sale at least half the time - don't get excited about sales on these items - 50% off is usually a good sale price on private labels.

- Brand names are on sale 25% percent of the time - 35 to 45% off is usually a good sale price on brand names.

- Wait and Watch – new merchandise is usually displayed 30 days before it is put on sale - if there is something you want, watch and see how fast it moves - if it doesn't move fast, it will probably be discounted.

- Buying clothes on sale for later use can be risky (potential style changes, weight changes…) - there are some items though you can probably safely purchase in advance such as socks, underwear, tennis shoes, etc.

- Avoid high traffic areas - this is where "in" merchandise, highest markups are - bargains are in the back of the department.

- General Dateline Guide - holiday/seasonal stuff comes out two months in advance, so retailers need to get rid of other stuff then. Spring clothing closeouts - End of April. Summer clothing closeout - end of July - Fall and back-to-school closeout - end of October - winter clothes closeout - end of January.

- Wait for year-end sales - getting rid of inventory for tax purposes is a real incentive for clothing stores.

- Accessorize instead of buying a new wardrobe.

- Rummage Sales / Garage Sales - go to the ones in better neighborhoods – they tend to throw out clothing before they wear out clothing – let someone else's change in taste be your bonanza!

- Swap clothes with friends or relatives.

- Ever wonder where dryer lint comes from? Its caused by fabric of clothes rubbing against other clothes and tumbling – you extend the life of clothing, especially fine clothing life by using a clothes line.

- Cut fabric softener sheets in half!

- Clothes fade less if washed inside out.

- Extend clothes life by turning inside out in dryer.

- Line dry often - string a line in the basement for the winter - clothes last longer and saves energy costs - 4 line-dry loads per week **saves $100 per year.**

- Invigorate the color in old jeans by washing them with new jeans - the dye that washes our from the new will soak into the old.

- Avoid dry-clean-only clothing

- Many dry-clean items can be hand washed instead - a frequently worn blouse that is hand-washed can **save $25 per year.**

- If you have a large amount of clothes that need to be dry-cleaned, find a cleaner that will charge a bulk per-pound rate.

- Buy imperfect of brands like L'eggs, Hanes, Bali, Playtex, etc. through the mail for 50% savings. The garments have minute flaws that you usually can't even find - **Save $50 per year.**

- A new nick in hose or stockings can be kept from running by applying nail polish to the spot - use uncolored!

- Alternate the shoes you wear each day - giving shoes a day to air out and dry greatly extends shoe life - use shoe trees or moisture from perspiration and rain will cause them to curl - cut your shoe expense in half by doubling their life!

- Polish shoes to extend life - without polishing, scuffmarks get etched into the leather and eventually crack.

- Driving ruins more shoes than walking! While moving foot to use gas and brake pedals, the back of the shoe gets worn down on carpeting - keep a pair of slip-ons in the car, especially when wearing dress shoes.

- Many shoes are ruined when they are placed close to heat source to dry - keep shoes away from heat source and stuff with newspaper to dry.

- Shoe repair is worth it - replace heels not shoes.

- Save shoes by using nylon "taps".

- Keep a pair of old shoes in the garage for doing yard work.

CHAPTER TWELVE
FOOD/GROCERY

According to the Statistical Abstract of the United States, the average family spends $4000 to $5000 per year on groceries. If you have a family, and choose to only focus on one area of spending, this is one area you can get the largest return on your Spend Smart investment of time.

With a little effort and planning, you can save $1000 per year on groceries!

Now if you can save this kind of money with ½ hour to 1 hour per week of preparation, that's like getting paid $20 to $40 per hour. Of course we know, that because of the Replacement Value of a Dollar, saving $1000 per year on grocery spending has the same financial impact as earning $1410 dollars. If you can earn $28 to $56 per hour by using Spend Smart in the grocery store, isn't that worth your time?

Now I bet some of you are expecting this section to be a big discussion on coupons. You've heard it all before…save $500/year using coupons! Well folks, the fact of the matter is:

Coupons can actually cause you to spend more money rather than Spend Smart!

Coupons can give the illusion of a good deal - they can lead to buying things or amounts you wouldn't have normally bought - coupons are often designed to encourage impulse buying - and once you buy something, the hope is you'll be more likely to buy it again.

Now we do believe that coupons can be good Spend Smart weapons in certain situations, but you can usually get better results from weekly specials. These store coupons usually have greater value than manufacturer coupons. We'll talk more about coupons later, but for now, we suggest a coupon strategy as follows:

Don't assume that the item with the coupon is the best buy for you.

- A different item could be a better value even without a coupon.

The best way to use coupons is a double whammy.

- If you have both a national brand coupon and a store coupon for the same item (usually you can use both, just not two of the same type of coupon on the same item).
- If you have a coupon and some rebate offer.

Store coupons are often very good coupon values.

- Doesn't take much time to get them from the paper.
- You don't have to keep them long because usually they are only good for a week.

National brand coupons are usually the worst coupon values.

- Usually, they aren't worth the bother.

Coupons - you can love them or hate them - many people don't like the hassle of cutting them out, keeping them, finding them when you need them, etc. For those who don't like the hassle of clipping and managing coupons, you still can save significant amounts of money on your groceries by following two simple rules:

1) **Stop shopping for brands and start shopping for bargains.**

Drop your loyalty to certain brands - Brand loyalty is usually developed through advertising - and you pay for the advertising via higher prices - be willing to try other lower-priced brands, especially store brands. More and more items are available as store brand and this can save you at least 20%. If you decide the quality of the name brand is so much better that you can't live without it, fine. If we were to conduct a taste test however, and have someone try a bowl of

Kellogg's Frosted flakes and a bowl of Store Brand Frosties, they couldn't tell the difference. On the other hand, they probably would notice saving as much as $1.50 per box.

2) **Plan your meals and menus around weekly store specials.**

Sometimes this means using store coupons, but they are only good for a week or two so you don't have to worry about the hassles of keeping them. Shopping and eating the sales can cut your food bills a good 25% - saves time too - you don't have to dig through your recipes and make decisions. You can buy 80% of the food needed for the coming week from weekly specials.

These two simple rules can help you save more money than most of the people who religiously use all coupons. For those of you willing to go the extra mile and get real value from a serious couponing effort, there are many books on the subject. If you want to accomplish even more than typical couponing achieves, depending on what your Spend Smart goals are, there is much more you can do to save money on food. First, it is helpful to understand the grocery business.

Know the Supermarket Game

- Supermarkets are selling machines - the wonderful smells from the bakery are designed to make you hungry - when you are hungry you make more unplanned purchases, hence you buy high profit items.

- Frequently purchased items (milk, eggs) are typically at the rear so you have to pass many appealing products and displays on the way (how often have you been able to "just get bread and milk"?

- Products at eye-level are often the most expensive - they are placed there because people most often pick the items that are at eye-level - low priced items are often low on the shelf.

- Grocers don't have a flat markup - variable pricing is used - different items have different markups - goal is to get people in the door with low-price items and make a profit on others - if you buy many non-sale items you give back the discount you came in for.

- The less frequently an item is purchased, the better the chance it has high markup. Consumer's don't know the difference between a good price or high price on items they don't buy often.

Supermarkets expect 2% profit, but they can sell items below cost for several reasons.

- They use loss leaders on "necessities" such as bread, milk, eggs to get people in to the store - they hope to make up their losses on other items you purchase.

- Stores get "Ad money" from manufacturers that allows them to sale price and have their own coupons.

- With good Spend Smart habits, you can identify the "below cost" items and achieve 25% discounts or more on much of what you buy.

- From a money-saving perspective, it is worth being familiar with the pricing habits of different stores in your area. We don't expect people to shop different stores every week, but we do suggest going to different stores at least several times a year to learn which have what staples at the lowest prices.

- If you don't have at least two major grocery stores nearby, choose a store that tends towards everyday low prices instead of a few super-sale items.

SPEND SMART TOP 10 GROCERY STRATEGIES

#1 - Never Shop Without a List.

To gain the most savings, you must have a game plan - make your plan according to the weekly specials - your list is your plan. Without a list, you will be much more influenced by marketing strategies which encourage you to purchase higher profit items.

- Food companies spend more than 7 billion dollars a year on advertising.

- Studies have shown that most shoppers make 2/3 of their purchase decisions in the store, often spending twice what they anticipated.

Without a list you will make more impulse buys and spend much more money, PERIOD!

2 - Know a Good Price.

This is a skill you need to use every time you shop because it only develops over time. 20% of the items highlighted in the specials are at or close to normal prices - you don't want to fall victim to the illusion of a good deal. You want to shoot for items that are 25% off or more.

- Use the Price Scoreboard – see your workbook - It's the only way you can remember many prices over time and it will help you more accurately assign a DealQ.

- Don't assume bigger packages are a better deal better. Sometimes small and medium size packages sell faster, so stores will accept a lower profit margin on them. Pay attention to unit pricing.

3 - Buy High Value Sale Items in the Largest Quantity Possible.

- The goal is to never pay full price.

- The more you stock up when the prices are low, the less you'll need when prices are high.

- Meat consumes about a third of the food budget so a stand-alone freezer lets you stock up on protein at sale prices.

4 – StockPile Items Before You Need Them.

When you wait to buy things until you need them, your ability to save money is decreased because "Just Saying No" is not an option. When you can buy three-month supplies of items, especially those you use frequently, you have much greater purchasing control.

Ultimately, if you can purchase items when the price is best instead of when your need is greatest, you will pay the lowest possible prices for your groceries, all the time.

- If you see an item you use a lot at the lowest price in three months, buy a three month supply - by the time your supply is used up, the sale price probably will have returned.

- If you can't afford to do this as often as you would like, focus on stock-piling expensive items (meat, cheese, peanut butter, coffee) or items you buy frequently because they will give you the greatest total savings.

- Keep your freezer 2/3rds full so you have room for unexpected bargains - fill the other 1/3 with plastic bottles of water.

- If you have a small freezer, use as much of your space for meat and cheese - save space by not buying frozen vegetables, dinners, etc. The space is much more valuable for expensive items you can stock up on when on sale.

5 - Be Careful about Buying Non-Food Items at Grocery Stores.

Though there can be exceptions to this rule depending on specials, items like paper products, pet food, toiletries, soaps, etc. can usually be found at better prices elsewhere (Target, K-mart, Wal-Mart), etc. It's ironic…Grocery stores get you in with low prices on food and try to make money on things like toothpaste. Target gets you in with low prices on toothpaste and tries to make money on food!

6 - Join a Warehouse Club.

Of course, you can get great buys on items in bulk, but you must be cautious - the atmosphere of places like Sam's Club can lead to bad spending decisions. People tend to assume all prices are great - impulse buying can go wild.

- Make sure you pay attention to per-ounce pricing because package sizes are often different than the typical sizes found in grocery stores.

- Don't join a warehouse if your annual purchases won't be more than 20 times the cost of the membership fee - for example, if the fee is $30, unless you think you'll spend more than $600 annually, the additional time and savings probably aren't worth it.

7 - Buy Store Brands.

Many products such as canned vegetables, cereal, condiments, etc. have 3 types of products - National Brand Names, Store Brands and Economy Brands. Though the price for an item can vary greatly between brands, the fact is, these products must meet the same FDA requirements and are basically the same. Ironically, many of the National Brand Name products actually make the store and generic brands - they just put different labels on the products!

- National brands are most expensive - with cereal 30% of the price covers the food - 20% covers the profits - the other 50% pays for advertising, promotions, coupons, etc.

- Store brands are typically the same quality as national brands. Store-brands don't have to compete for shelf space (Cub's going to put their products on their shelves right?) so they spend much less on advertising. Store brand products are typically at least 20% less than the equal quality national brand. Even if you have a coupon for the national brand, store brands are usually a better deal!

- Economy brands (like Flavorite, Shur-Fine, Best-Yet) often cost 20 to 40% less, but they can be lower quality or irregularly sized - food is safe and meets FDA standards - it just may not be as pleasing to your taste buds.

8 - Watch the Cash Register Like its Your Money (Because it is!)

- A 1993 investigation by Money magazine found that because of scanner errors, as many as 30% of supermarkets may overcharge their customers (see Appendix D).

- The stores Money caught overcharging did it on about 10% of items. So if you don't watch carefully as your items are rung up, some sneaky scanner may eat your lunch.

- Better yet, some stores give you the item for free if it rings up wrong (All the more reason to watch!).

9 - Avoid Prepared Foods.

Prepared foods include items like frozen dinners, vegetables in cheese sauce, canned stews, boil and serve and hot foods from the deli. While these items are convenient, you pay for that convenience in two ways:

- Higher price - usually two to three times as expensive as making it yourself.

- Lower nutrition - prepared foods have lost a great deal of the nutrition found in vegetables, etc, even when compared to canned vegetables.

- If you like the convenience, when you cook, make double batches and freeze half of it for future convenience.

 # 10 - Learn to Substitute Ingredients and Experiment.

If a recipe calls for a spice you rarely use or don't have, substitute something else or omit the item - this helps avoid trips to get a single item - saves time and money because most people can't go to the store and just get one item. Refer to the following substitution list as a good place to start.

Substitutions

ITEM	SUBSTITUTE
1 cup of buttermilk or sour cream	1 cup of milk with 1 Tbs vinegar or lemon juice
1 cup of sour cream	1 cup plain yogurt
1 cup brown sugar	1 cup sugar mixed with 1 Tbs molasses
Any kind of nut	equal amount of cheaper nut (almonds for walnuts)
Nuts in cookie recipes	Oatmeal
1 cup of honey	1 cup sugar plus ¼ cup water
1 cup corn syrup	1 cup sugar and ¼ cup water
1 square of baking chocolate	3 Tbs cocoa powder and 1 Tbs butter
1 Tbs cornstarch	2 Tbs flour
Cooking wine	inexpensive table wine
1 cup heavy cream	¾ cup milk and 1/3 cup butter
1 cup light cream	¾ cup milk and 3 Tbs butter
1 tsp lemon juice	½ tsp plain vinegar
Whipped cream	Beat a ripe banana and egg white
Bread crumbs	grind up crackers

BEVERAGES

- Don't buy juice in cans or bottles, especially individual servings - if the kids like the fun of the individual servings, you can buy little "flip-top" containers that serve the same purpose - buy frozen concentrate.

- Kids really like Kool-Aid as much as pop - Kool-Aid costs about 20 cents per quart including sugar - pop at $5.00 a case costs about 2 cents an ounce compared to about ½ cent per ounce for Kool-Aid - pop is 4 times as expensive! Besides, Kool-Aid even has some vitamins and there's no artificial sweeteners or caffeine! If you replace a 12 pack of pop per week with Kool-Aid, **save $94 per year.**

- If you must buy pop, never pay more than $4.00 per case for brand names or $.90 for a two-liter bottle. Stores often use soda as a loss leader to get you in the door. Better yet, buy Shasta or Chex, the off-brand pops.

CEREAL

- Beware of cereal! Even with a $1.00 off coupon, it is not unusual for brand cereal to be more than $3.00 a box. Never pay more than $2.00 per box for cereal. Most of the popular cereal gets rotated through weekly specials where you can get Lucky Charms, Cheerios, Captain Crunch, etc. for this price or even better if you have a manufacturer's coupon.

- If you can't wait for the sale, Store Brands and Malt-o-Meal cereals (in the bag) have the comparable product at $2.00 or less.

- If your kids think they have to have the brand name, do the Roseanne trick - keep the box from a brand name and put the bag from the store brand in it - they'll never know the difference!

- Cereal price per ounce comparison (at retail):

	Brand name	Store brand
Cornflakes	17¢	7¢
Honey oats	25¢	11¢
Sweet Puffed Wheat	14¢	8¢

- Average size of a box of cereal is 20 oz - if you save 10 cents an ounce, you save $2.00 per box - for every box of cereal your family eats each week, **save $100 per year.**

COUPONS

- Manufacturer Coupons can cause you to spend more! Usually manufacturers coupons won't get you a better buy than the store brands unless they are on sale too.

- Coupons and rebates can be good if used wisely, but consider the time involved - people who spend as much as eight hours a week managing coupons can get 25% to 30% savings (about a $3.00 hourly wage) but you can get the same savings without the time involved by planning your meals around the weekly specials.

- Store coupons can be the best coupon values. They are usually only good for a week so you don't have to collect them and keep track of them. Even if you don't want to collect coupons, spend 15 minutes going over the Sunday newspaper ads to plan your shopping and grab the store coupons before you go.

- In most areas, at least one store sends out a 2-week coupon book in the mail with unadvertised specials. While the coupons usually have a purchase limit, if you go to the store more than once in the two-week period, ask for one of the coupon books at the service desk. That way you can use the best coupons every time you go to the store.

- Look for double whammies - items where you have both a store coupon and a national brand coupon - often you can use both!

- Always bring your coupons when you shop - if you see an unadvertised special you might be able to "double down".

- Organize coupons into categories if you plan on saving them - dairy, baby, drinks, paper, meat, snacks, cereal, baking, pets, canned goods, frozen food, hygiene, miscellaneous.

- Put an asterisk next to each coupon item on your list so you don't forget to use it.

DAIRY

- Never buy a dairy product without checking expiration date – grab the items from the back of the shelf because their expiration date is usually farther into the future.

- Shredded or sliced cheese usually costs more, unless bought in bulk - compare price per ounce costs.

- Buy cheaper ice cream - usually more healthy too because it has less fat.

- Try Powdered Milk - If you don't like the taste, make a 50/50 mixture of powdered milk and regular milk. For every gallon of milk you replace each week with powdered milk, **save $50 per year.**

MEAT

- 1/3 of the food budget is spent on meat - we eat 50% more meat than the Recommended Daily Allowance says we need to – making casseroles, stews and soups will cut your meat budget while still meeting your health requirements.

- When meat is a main course - serve small portions served with lots of filling but inexpensive side dishes such as potatoes, pasta, rice and salads - stir-fry is another good meat-stretcher.

- Regard all meat as expensive - try to use meat as an ingredient, not the meal (casseroles, soup, etc.).

- Use bread crumbs as a great meat extender - add bread crumbs (it's easy to make your own) to sloppy joes, meat loaf, tacos, etc. - you can even buy leaner more expensive ground beef, add bread crumbs, and still save money if you want. Assuming a price of $1.49 per pound (average for regular, lean and extra lean ground beef) If you use 2 pounds of ground beef per week at 1.49/pound average price for all grades, with extender, you **save $75 per year.**

- Try chicken thighs as a great low-cost alternative to chicken breast meat - they are easy to bone out. For every pound of chicken breast meat you replace with chicken thigh meat per week (breast at 2.49/pound and thigh at 1.09/pound) you **save $70 per year.**

- Paying more for brand name chicken is not justified - all chicken meets the same FDA standards - price per pound - consider too that with whole chickens, you have about 50% bones and fat - thighs have the least amount of either - therefore, thighs at 79 cents a pound are a better bargain than whole chickens at 49 cents per pound.

- Consumer Reports test of over 35 brands of bacon found little difference in taste - they recommend buying by price.

- Frying thin strips of ham is healthier and more economical than bacon.

- Be careful if you buy a side of beef - the weight is "hanging weight" meaning half of it will be bone and trimmings.

- Buy meat seasonally - better cuts of beef cost more during the summer because demand is high during the cookout season.

- Like Rib Eye - Chuck is right next to it and comes from the same muscle group, but Chuck is the half price.

- Don't buy Deli meat - buy a whole pre-cooked ham or turkey breast and ask them to slice it for you (usually no charge).

- Consider the weight of the bone when buying meat - often, it is cheaper to go boneless.

- Marinade less expensive cuts - they are great not just for flavor, but they tenderize as well. Less expensive cuts (round, etc.) come from the bottom of the animal - they are tougher because they are more active muscle - more expensive cuts come from the muscles on top of the animal which are more tender from less use. Longer marinating time gives better results.

- MARINADE RECIPE - for cheap cuts of beef - ¼ c. oil, ¼ c. wine vinegar, ¼ c soy sauce, ¼ c chopped onion, 1 tsp. Garlic salt, 1 tsp basil, 1 tsp. Salt, 1 tsp pepper, ½ tsp. Ginger.

- CHILD-PLEASER MARINADE RECIPE - 1 ½ c tomato juice, ½ c chopped onion, 2 Tbs wine vinegar, 1 clove minced garlic, 1 tsp salt, ½ tsp hot pepper sauce.

- MARINADE RECIPE - for chicken or beef - ½ c soy sauce, ¼ c honey, ½ tsp garlic powder OR ¼ c Worcestershire, 1 Tbs minced onion, 2 Tbs lemon juice, 2 Tbs oil, 1-tsp salt, ½ tsp minced garlic.

MISCELLANEOUS

- EATING OUT – in the 1970s – 20% of household food money was spent on eating out – in the 1990s that figure has doubled to 40%! The average bill for a family of four eating out is $31. A comparable dinner can be made at home for $7. Eat out one time less per month and **save $288 per year!**

- Stay away from vending machines at work. Little things add up. Average vending machine users spend $1.20 three times a week - bring a thermos if you pay for coffee - buy snacks on sale and keep them in your desk - **save $180 per year.**

- Brown bag your lunch to work a few times a week - sandwich, apple, can of pop, several snacks will cost you 1.50 - same food out costs $5 to $6 -

for each day/per week you brown bag instead of eating out, **save $200 per year.**

- Next to meat, nothing gouges your food budget as much as snacks - cookies, candy, chips, flavored crackers can cost much - best idea is to keep these out of the house as much as possible - rely on popcorn, peanut butter/jelly toast, pretzels, graham crackers, fruit, etc. as snacks.

- If you often need a chocolate fix, stock up after holidays (Easter, Halloween, Valentines Day, Christmas) when holiday candy is 50% off.

- Avoid gourmet popcorn - national and store brands taste as good at half the price.

- Consider joining a buying club - To locate a co-op or buying club, call the National Cooperative Business Association at 800-636-6222 (press 2, then 2 when prompted to) and leave your name and address. The association will send you a list of regional warehouses that supply co-ops; the warehouse nearest you can then refer you to outlets in your area. How much will you save? According to the co-op association, about 33% to 49% off normal supermarket prices, with the biggest savings coming at the buying clubs.

- Join the SHARE food coop/volunteer program (See appendix B) – **save at least $192 per year.**

- Use the Price Scorecard in your workbook as a tracking list of good prices on the 50 items you buy most frequently - start out by writing down what you think is a good price on the item, then write down the month and price when you see it at a better price.

- Watch egg prices - size IS important - X-Large eggs = 27 ounces - Large eggs = 24 ounces - Medium eggs = 21 ounces - Small eggs = 18ounces - if the price difference is 10% or less between sizes, buy the larger size.

- Store bought frozen pancakes, french toast and waffles are filled with expensive air - next time you make them from scratch, make extra and freeze them - pop them into the microwave when you want instant pancakes.
- Flavored noodle or rice mixes are expensive - make your own basic cheese sauce - mix 1 cup instant nonfat milk, 3 Tbs grated cheese (Romano, Parmesan or Cheddar), 1/3 cup dried minced onions, 1 Tbs garlic powder, ½ tsp salt, ½ tsp pepper - to use, combine ¼ cup of mixture with ¼ cup milk and 2 Tbs butter - pour over cooked noodles - keep in an airtight container, this mixture keeps on your shelf for 4 months.

- Healthy eating is (usually) the same as low-cost eating - beans, potatoes, bananas, oranges, apples, rice, oats, flour…they all cost under 60 cents per pound.

- Do not shop when you are hungry - leads to impulse buying and convenience food buying.

- Check per-ounce pricing, usually listed on the price tag on the shelf to compare prices - this can be important because sometimes, the larger quantity does not save money - it may even cost money if you have a coupon for a smaller size.

PRODUCE

- Don't buy vegetables in little bags with cheese sauce - make your own sauce or use cheese soup.

- Once bananas reach their desired ripeness, place them in the refrigerator - the skin will blacken but the fruit will be fine.

- Ingredients for stews, casseroles, soups needn't always be of the highest quality - economy-brand vegetables may often be irregularly sized, but does it matter in a stew - save the 20 to 40% over the name brand.

FOOD PREPARATION

- Though microwaves are inexpensive in terms of energy use, "microwave-able" foods however are expensive.
- Dead bananas - freeze, peel and all for banana bread, peanut butter/banana sandwiches, add to cookie dough for half of shortening, make shakes.

- Brew Iced Tea - three tea bags in two quarts of water - microwave on high for 10 minutes. Better yet – make Sun Tea!

- Make bread crumbs - great hamburger extender - do not throw away old bread - toast anything not hard and dry - put in blender to make crumbs - buy day old bread to do this.

- Make spaghetti sauce - buy spaghetti sauce seasoning - mix with tomato sauce - add your own ingredient fresh (green peppers, mushrooms, ground beef, etc.

- When cooking pasta, bring salted water to a boil, add pasta, turn off heat - pasta will be perfectly cooked in 12 to 15 minutes.

FOOD STORAGE

- Freeze meat in the portion size you want so you don't have to unthaw a bulk package all at once.

- Meat loses nutritional value after six months in the freezer – don't buy more than a six-month supply!

- Make your own frozen dinners - make double batches and freeze single portion servings for future use.

CHAPTER THIRTEEN
HOLIDAYS/GIFT
GIVING/CHRISTMAS

It seems even the most dedicated Spend Smart student can have trouble at holiday times. Madison Avenue advertising has convinced us that it won't be a great holiday unless we SPEND, SPEND, SPEND! Just like with spending on children, think of the long-term perspective. Gifts are usually forgotten shortly after they are received. The gift of financial security for your family will endure for a lifetime. Which is more important to you?

- The gift of time and attention is the most appreciated - make up fancy certificates pledging your time to baby-sit, clean house, give back rubs, cook, take someone fishing, etc.

- Take the time to help your kids appreciate the spirit of giving – let them pick a gift to give to some charity.

- Always keep a gift list so you can buy gifts on sale throughout the year, for birthdays, Christmas, etc.

- Want to save potentially hundreds of dollars? Celebrate the religious holiday at Christmas time - do gift buying, etc. the week after Christmas and have present time on New Years! I know this one is a little radical… Typical Christmas spending is $700 per family. Buy everything the week after Christmas and **save $350 per year.**

- Give value by giving gift certificates for Christmas - a dollar will purchase twice as much merchandise the week after Christmas plus you can make sure people get what they want!

- Best time to shop for next Christmas is the week after this Christmas - hit the sales and buy next year's presents, wrapping paper, ornaments/lights, cards, etc.
- Recycle Christmas Cards. Take the cards you receive and cut off the front cover. Send it as a Christmas postcard next year - the cards you

send will all be different but you'll save up to 50 cents per card including the 12 cents difference on postage between a postcard and a first class letter. If you send 75 cards, **save $38 per year.**

- Do Christmas shopping all throughout the year or wait until the last two days before Christmas.

> # CHAPTER FOURTEEN
> ## HOUSEHOLD

Household items usually are consumable items. That is, you use what you have and then you buy more. In this area, the Spend Smart Strategies focus on using less and using substitutes.

- Disposable means expensive - Use rags instead of paper towels.

- Buy product refills instead of new products – that way you don't pay for a new container each time.

- Price per ounce is not a good measure in cleaning products – what's important is how good something cleans – which product offers the best cleaning power for the dollar. Where is the best value?

- Take Inventory of all the cleaners you have under sinks, in cupboards, in closets before you buy any more.

- Make your own cleaners - primary ingredient in most cleaners is ammonia.

  WARNING - treat any cleaner containing ammonia carefully! Without proper ventilation, ammonia can irritate the eyes and lungs. ALSO, don't mix ammonia with bleach or commercial cleansers because the interaction can form dangerous fumes!

Cleaning Product Recipes

- all-purpose Cleaner (Like Formula 409) - 14 cups warm water - add 1 cup washing soda and 1 cup ammonia - put in spray bottle and apply undiluted to spot clean tiles, counters, metal, porcelain - use 1 cup cleaner in bucket of warm water for large jobs - costs about 60 cents a gallon compared to $15 gallon of name-brand cleaner.

- Milder cleaner - 2 tsps borax and 1 Tbs liquid detergent to 1 quart of warm water - put in spray bottle.

- Dishwasher detergent - 3 cups borax, 3 cups washing soda, 1/8 cup powdered laundry detergent.

- Disinfectant spray (like Lysol) - mix ½ chlorine bleach with 3-½ cups water - costs 10 cents versus $5 for name brand spray.

- Tile/Grout/Porcelain cleaner (like Soft Scrub) - - 14 cups warm water - add 1 cup baking soda, 1 cup ammonia, ½ cup white vinegar - or just use 1 part bleach and 3 parts water - 15 cents a quart versus $4.00.

- Toilet bowl cleaner - use all-purpose cleaner above.

- Detergent for wool and delicate garments (like Woolite) - just use the same liquid detergent you'd use for hand washing dishes - 1 tsp per quart of water.

- Ingredients like borax, ammonia and washing soda can usually be found at a drug store.

MISCELLANEOUS

- Dust Spray - you don't need Endust (though it smells good!) – just use a slightly damp rag.

- Ant and cockroach killer - 2 cups borax and 1 cup flour (store in glass jar - punch holes in the cover) - sprinkle around the outside foundation of the house - inside on along baseboards and door sills - pour some in jar lids left under the sink and in cupboards.

HEALTH AND BEAUTY PRODUCTS

- Take inventory of your bathroom shelves before you buy more.

- To whiten fingernails, soak in lemon juice then brush with a 50/50 white vinegar / warm water rinse.

- Remove make-up easily with baby oil or petroleum jelly.

- Blemish Cream? - dab pimple with lemon juice several times a day to dry it out.

- Find a beauty salon that will trim neck and bangs between cuts for free.

- Cut your kids hair yourself – you can get hair clippers, barber's scissors and instructional video for about $20. A typical kids haircut is $8 – if they get a haircut 4 times a year, for each child you have (they'll usually only let you cut their hair while they are in grade school) **save $32 per year.**

| **CHAPTER FIFTEEN** |
| **INSURANCE** |

Insurance is the area in most people's finances that they spend the most amount of money on but they understand the least. The average American family spends $2,000 to $5,000 per year on insurance. Outside of debt, for most people, this is where Spend Smart can help them save the greatest amount of money.

Spend Smart students believe that insurance is a very valuable asset. We also believe it is important to have the right coverages for the right purpose. As with all areas of spending, buying something you don't need is a terrible waste of money.

Insurance can have such a dramatic impact on people's financial life, both in terms of the amount of money spent and in terms of the money you receive in times of financial crisis. Therefore it is extremely important that you become as educated as possible about insurance. Don't simply rely on what you learn from Spend Smart about insurance.

Do your own research. Go the library or bookstore and you will find dozens of books designed to help the average person understand insurance better. Information and education are two of your most powerful Spend Smart Strategies!

First it is important that you understand some basic concepts regarding insurance...

Spend Smart Laws of Insurance

1. **The purpose of Insurance is to protect you from catastrophe, not inconvenience.**

   You should insure yourself against large or catastrophic losses - ones that could wipe you out financially - don't insure losses that you can afford to pay out of your pocket. You'll pay much more in premium than you need to if you expect insurance to pay for everything.

2. When you buy Insurance, you (almost) always lose financially.

For most of us, we will pay far more in premiums than we ever receive back in claim payments. When you think about it however, that's good. While you're happy to have the security of insurance, do you really want to collect? Would you really want to:

- Collect a settlement because your house burned down?

- Get a new car because yours was totaled?

- Have your heirs receive a $250,000 death benefit?

All insurance can do is protect us from financial loss and hardship. Major loss takes an emotional toll that cannot be compensated for. Insurance companies are designed to be profitable, to make money based on the odds of misfortune - it's similar to gambling in that only a few people come out ahead (receive more in claims than paid in premium). None-the-less, we need insurance, "just in case".

3. When Buying Insurance, You Should Assume as Much Risk as Possible.

Assuming risk means be willing to cover more of the smaller losses out of your pocket rather than ask the insurance company to pay for them. Why would you do this - wouldn't it be great if they paid for everything?

NO - one of the biggest costs insurance companies have is the administrative cost of processing and paying a claim. This cost is a constant, it is the same whether your claim is for $250 or $2500. The more claims you file, the greater the company's cost.

When you have a low dollar (say $250) deductible as compared to a high dollar deductible (say $1000), an insurance company's potential cost is increased in two ways. First, they will have to pay more in the case a claim is filed (everything beyond $250). Second, they will have more administrative costs because more claims will be filed with a lower deductible.

By raising deductibles, you increase the amount of loss you assume responsibility for. This decreases the potential cost to the insurance company. This decreased cost is passed on to you in the form of lower premiums.

4. Avoid Wasting Money on Duplicate Coverage and Specialty Coverage.

Duplicate coverage exists when two or more policies cover the same person for the same loss. For example, perhaps you and your spouse both have health insurance through work. Insurance laws dictate that you cannot profit from a loss - therefore, you cannot be paid from two different policies for the same loss. Hence, duplicate coverage is a complete waste of money.

Avoid specialty policies or policies with narrow coverage (flight insurance, cancer policies, towing rider on your auto insurance, etc.) - There is a fixed cost of issuing and maintaining a policy. You pay this costs will all policies so the fewer policies you have by combining coverage, the better. Here's what your policies should cover in general.

- Health insurance should cover all diseases.

- Disability insurance should replace regular income.

- Life insurance should pay off all your bills and provide income without buying separate credit insurance.

- Auto insurance should cover you when you drive any vehicle, including rentals.

AUTO INSURANCE

Auto insurance is the largest insurance expense for most families. People tend to overpay for auto insurance because they buy the same type of coverage they have always bought and assume their needs never change. Let's look at some powerful Spend Smart Strategies for auto insurance:

- Raise your auto deductible from $200 to $500 for collision and comprehensive coverage and you can save as much as 30% on your premium. With the national average annual auto insurance premium of $1000, raising your auto insurance premium can **save you $300 per car, per year.**

- Avoid specialty coverage like emergency road service, towing, specialty coverage of audio equipment - this is insuring losses you can afford to cover yourself - losing proposition - **save $50 per year.**

- Avoid policies that duplicate coverage - don't buy medical coverage through your auto policy (other than the state minimum required amounts). The general health policy is a better value and already covers such health problems.

- When the blue book value on your vehicle sinks to $2000 or less, consider dropping collision and comprehensive insurance. People think collision and comprehensive insurance will replace their car if totaled. NOT TRUE! If your car is totaled, you will be paid the auction value (this is less than the trade-in value) less your deductible. This will not replace your car. Save money with the decreased premium and assume the risk yourself. **Save $500 per year!**

- Only file claims for more than $500 in damage - when you file claims, rates will be raised - don't use the insurance, just because you have it - use it when you need it!

- Drivers under age 26 have highest rates - if a parent is paying the bill, put their car in your name and on your policy to save large amounts of premium - of course, if they have an accident, that will hurt your insurance.

- Don't assume that just because one company has good rates for your friend that you will get good rates as well. Rates vary within a company from driver to driver depending on whether they are male or female, age, driving history, type of car, amount of driving, profession, etc.

- Shop around for price quotes every year, even if you have a good rate now – WHY? Auto insurance rates are updated at least every year. These rates reflect how much the company paid in claims last year. Ever had your rates go up, even though you didn't have an accident? Your rates with another company might go down if their loss experience is less than your current company.

Every company has different prices in different areas at different times - some of the companies that consistently offer the best rates include:

- Aetna (203-273-0123)
- AIG (800-807-9458)
- GEICO (301-986-3000)
- USAA (800-531-8319) - for people on active or reserve military duty and their children
- USF&G (301-547-3000)

What coverage do you need? All states have minimum coverage requirements. In Minnesota, for example, the minimum coverage requirements are:

- personal liability - $30,000 per person / $60,000 per accident.
- personal injury - $20,000.
- property damage (to others) - $10,000.
- Under/uninsured motorist - $25,000 per person / $50,000 per accident.

- It is recommended you have liability insurance equal to the amount of your net worth - in today's lawsuit-happy society, you can be taken for everything you have. Have minimum on injury because your health insurance covers you there.

- If you have a large net worth, you should consider getting umbrella liability coverage - costs around $200/ year for $1,000,000 coverage - purpose is to protect your assets from lawsuits.

- Cost of insurance is different with different makes and models of cars - don't believe what car salesmen tell you about the cost - call your agent to make sure.

- The Insurance Institute for Highway Safety's free booklet "Injury, Collision & Theft Losses" tells which recent models have racked up better or worse insurance claims. (For a copy write to Publications, P.O. Box 1420, Arlington, VA 22210).

Get every last discount you're entitled to. Discounts vary from state to state and company to company, but the following list of discounts, based mostly on information provided by State Farm, will give you a notion of what's out there:

Note that an auto insurance policy is made up of a number of different coverages (two of them, collision and comprehensive, together account for about half of the premium), and discounts often apply to some coverages but not to others.

- Accident-free. After three years without a chargeable accident, policyholders get a 10% break on collision, comprehensive and several other coverages; after six years, the discount rises to 15%.

- Multiple automobile. Insuring more than one car with the same company can mean a discount of 15% on most coverages.

- Short annual mileage. If you drive your car less than 7,500 miles a year, you may get about 15% off.

- Low "damage-ability". That's insurance jargon for a car that's statistically less likely to result in an expensive claim, either because it's cheaper to repair or less appealing to car thieves. Typical discount: 10% to 30% off collision and comprehensive premiums.

- Good student. Discounts of up to 25% are available to unmarried drivers under age 25 who rank in the top 20% of their class, have at least a B average or the equivalent, or are on the dean's list or honor roll at their high school or college. If the student is off at school more than 100 miles away, ask about an additional discount.

- Age 50. If you're 50 or older (with no unmarried drivers under 25 hanging around the house), you can get 10% off the usual adult rate.

- Defensive driving course. If you complete a course sponsored by your state, you'll often be eligible for a discount, usually around 5%. This discount frequently applies only to drivers age 55 and up.

- Passive restraints. If your car has airbags or automatic seatbelts, you'll save up to 40% on some coverages. Antilock brakes will also get you a break (commonly about 5%) at some insurers and in some states.

- Non-commuter. Driving less than 30 miles a week to and from work will earn you a 15% discount off the rate paid by drivers who rack up 100 or more miles. If you participate in a carpool, you may also be eligible for a discount.

- Anti-Theft devices. Depending on your state and the type of device, you could save up to 15% of your comprehensive premium. (This discount is worth checking out before you sink a lot of money into a security system).

PROPERTY/HOMEOWNER INSURANCE

- Raise Your Deductibles. The Insurance Information Institute, an industry group, says raising a $250 deductible to $500 will typically save you up to 12% on your homeowners premium. Average homeowner premium is $500. By raising your deductible to $500, the average homeowner can **save $48 per year.**

- A $1,000 deductible will save you 24%, and a $2,500 deductible as much as 30%. Raising deductibles this high, you can **save $120 to $150 per year.**

- Get rid of specialized coverages - they are often cover small risks - things you should cover yourself.

- Get replacement value coverage for home and contents - costs 10 to 15% more but because many items depreciate quickly, experts believe replacement value is a better value than market value coverage.

LIFE INSURANCE

Most people typically misunderstand life insurance. That's a shame because many people over-spend tens of thousands of dollars on life insurance over their lifetimes. Apply the Spend Smart laws of insurance, especially #1 – The purpose of insurance is to protect against catastrophe and #2 – You almost always lose financially.

It is important to first understand the specific purpose of life insurance. The general purpose is to replace the income of the person who dies. One way to look at life insurance is as a "guarantee" of completing one's financial plan. When the insured dies, if the insurance benefit is large enough, it can be invested and generate enough interest income each year to replace the income of the deceased.

Most people make the assumption they will always need life insurance. Hopefully however, as one's estate or net worth increases, the need for life insurance will decrease because the value of the estate can provide enough interest income to replace lost income.

Given the purpose for life insurance, let's look at who needs life insurance. This is important because Spend Smart advocates not buying products you don't need. Once you determine if life insurance might be something of value for you, then we'll look at different types of life insurance.

Who Needs Life Insurance?

The people who typically need life insurance are income earners with dependant children. If these income earners die, their life insurance should provide a lump sum of money which can be invested to produce interest income sufficient to replace lost income. A spouse who stays home with children, even if they don't earn an income, should be covered as well. If a spouse who is the primary caregiver for a couple's children dies, the other spouse would require additional income to provide childcare while the they continued to work. Others who need life insurance would include single-income couples where one spouse stays home and is dependent upon the other's income.

In general, from a personal finance perspective, these are the only types of people who need life insurance. Please be aware however, that there are specific circumstances where other factors determine a life insurance need such as business ownership, large estate management and income tax strategies. For the typical person, these scenarios do not come into play so these situations are not included in this overview.

Do children need life insurance?

10 to 15% of life insurance is sold to children. This doesn't seem to make much sense since they don't have dependents or income. Life insurance for

children is typically sold as a "savings plan" for college or on the basis of parents "caring about and loving" their children. We'll look more at this concept of using life insurance as a savings plan. You will see that if you are looking for an investment for college for your kids, it is difficult to think of any investment that costs more and gives you less of a return on your investment (premium) than life insurance.

Do single people need life insurance?

25% of all life insurance is sold to single. Single people don't need life insurance unless they have dependent children. Why would they need to replace their income (primary purpose of life insurance) if no one, other than themselves is dependent on it?

The insurance industry gives several reasons why singles and children should have life insurance. One argument says the earlier you start a life insurance policy, the lower your premiums will be. We'll see later how misleading this concept is, but for now realize just as there is no such thing as a "free lunch" in life, there are no "freebies" in life insurance. Another reason used to sell life insurance to children or single people is the concept of guaranteed insurability. You may not need insurance now, but you might in the future. Guaranteed insurability means you are guaranteed the right to buy insurance, even if you develop a terminal disease and wouldn't otherwise be eligible for life insurance. We'll see how this is misleading as well.

Types of Life Insurance

Though life insurance is sold in many different formats, all life insurance really just a variation of three basic types of life insurance: Term Life Insurance, Whole Life Insurance and Universal Life Insurance.

Term Life Insurance

Term Life Insurance is "plain vanilla" insurance. 100% of the premiums paid go into protection for your heirs. If premiums are discontinued than the coverage ends. It is the least expensive form of life insurance yet it does everything most people need a policy to do. Simply, it protect against the catastrophe of dependents losing their income source.

Whole Life Insurance

Whole Life Insurance is a combination of insurance and investment. A portion of the premium goes into what is known as "cash value" This is the most expensive form of life insurance because you overpay your premiums, at least in the early years of the policy. You pay much more than the cost of the insurance, sometimes as much as 1000% more to create the cash value. Whole Life is sold as an investment as well as insurance protection.

Universal Life Insurance

Universal Life Insurance combines insurance and investment. It is similar to term insurance in that the cost of insurance coverage is low cost. It is similar to Whole Life in that you overpay premiums to build an investment amount, like cash value. With Universal Life, you can choose the amount of money (within limits) that go to paying for the insurance and the amount that goes to build the investment portion of the policy.

Life Insurance Myths and Realities

Term Life Insurance is typically the least expensive type of insurance, often as much as 80 to 90% less in price, yet many people buy other types of life insurance. Why is this? Let's look at how Whole Life and Universal Life policies are presented so that people look at them in the most favorable light.

Myth #1 – Whole Life Insurance is an Investment.

When you buy a Whole Life policy, you will pay the same premium every month and will have a fixed amount of death benefit. One stated benefit of Whole Life is that it's an insurance policy with an investment plan, the cash value that increases in value. Some of your premium goes into cash value so your cash value increases over time. Most people believe therefore, that the cash value is an additional amount of money your beneficiaries would receive, beyond the insurance amount or you would receive if you cancelled the policy.

Here's the ugly truth about Whole Life Insurance cash value. IT DOESN'T BELONG TO YOU! Cash Value is the property of the insurance company. Many people mistakenly think that if they have a $100,000 policy with a $20,000 cash value, and they die, their heirs will receive the insurance amount and the cash value, or a total of $120,000.

Here's what really happens with cash value. If you die, your beneficiary receives the insurance amount OR the cash value amount, which ever is larger, but they don't get both! So, with Whole Life, you spend years overpaying premium to build cash value, but the cash value doesn't belong to you and you don't get any of it! Does that sound like a Spend Smart way to buy life insurance?

Myth #2 – If you need money, you can borrow against the Whole Life cash value.

This is true, but again, it isn't as good as it sounds. People assume the cash value belongs to them and we know that's not true.

When you borrow against cash value, you are charged interest. Even though you typically expect to pay interest on a loan, this surprises people because they think "it's their money". Further, if you borrow against cash value, any loan that is not repaid is subtracted from your death benefit. SO, if you have a $100,000 whole life policy and you borrow $10,000 if you die before paying it back, your heirs only receive $90,000!

Myth # 3 – Universal Life Insurance is a good deal.

Universal Life Insurance was created in the early 1980s. Many upstart insurance companies were promoting a new alternative to Whole life. They proposed that you should take the money you would use for Whole Life premiums, buy an inexpensive Term Life policy and invest the remaining amount of money you would have spent on Whole Life. Universal Life insurance was positioned as being similar to Term Life because the insurance costs were low and similar to Whole Life but with more flexible and higher earning investment choices.

Spend Smart says that for most people, Universal Life is a better deal than Whole Life, but sales commission charges, administrative fees, etc. are very high. These expenses mean that your investment return in a Universal Life policy is typically much lower than it would be with a regular investment, like a mutual fund.

For example, if you spend $1200 a year on a Universal Life policy, the salesperson typically makes around an 80% commission, or $960. If you could buy the same amount of insurance in a Term Life policy for $200 dollars a year and invested the other $1000, you would probably only pay about $150 in commissions. If you want the most for your money, because of high sales costs and other reasons, you typically are better off separating your investments from your life insurance.

Myth #4 – Disappearing Premiums.

Some Universal Life policies are sold with the idea that your premium will eventually "disappear". The idea is that once the investment portion grows large enough, it will produce enough income to cover the premium cost. There are several problems with this. First, because of high expense charges, it can take a very long time for cash value to grow to this point. Returns quoted are often current rates which are typically much higher than guaranteed rates. Second, remember the investment portion of the policy, and any interest growth it builds, belongs to you in a Universal Life policy. It still is your money paying the premium – you just don't have to write a check for it each month!

Myth #5 – Term Insurance is not a Good Long Term Choice.

While it is true that the cost of term insurance goes up as you get older, this should come as no surprise because cost of any life insurance policy increases each year. The difference is in how the premiums are paid. While your Whole Life or Universal policy premium may stay the same every year, the insurance still costs more. The cash value or investment portion of the policy funds the increased costs. These extra costs as you get older are actually costs you have paid for in advance with higher-than-necessary premiums when you were younger.

Though term rates go up over time and eventually can become higher than Whole Life or Universal Life rates on policies you started years ago, the cost of insurance is based on your age and really is the same regardless of the type of policy you have. The Whole Life and Universal Life policies just avoid increasing your premiums by taking from the cash or investment value of the policy. Bottom line, when life insurance costs go up each year, you always pay for it – the difference is whether the additional cost comes directly from your pocket or from your earlier over-payment of premium.

A Final Word On Life Insurance

The authors of Spend Smart feel that Life Insurance is an essential portion of a sound financial plan. We just have two basic areas of disagreement with the life insurance industry in general. First, we believe in most cases, Term Life insurance provides the best value. Second, we believe that for most people, with good Spend Smart habits, you won't need life insurance for your entire life because you will be able to build investments large enough to replace your income.

ONE WORD OF CAUTION

If you currently have Whole Life or Universal Life Insurance – DON'T CANCEL THEM. First shop around for term rates. Look at the rates for 10, 20, 30 years into the future or however long you think you will need the coverage. When you find a policy that makes sense for you, apply for it. If you are accepted, then you can decide what to do with your existing Whole Life or Universal Life policy but the last thing you want to happen is to find out you can't get another Life Insurance policy after you have cancelled some.

Canceling a Whole Life or Universal Life policy usually wastes a great deal of money. Even if you want to stop paying premiums on these expensive policies, there are ways to get the maximum value from a policy while you stop paying on it. If you just cancel a policy, you may receive what is called a surrender value, but this is typically much less than the cash or investment value.

Consider a few options. Check with your agent and see how long your coverage will continue if you stop paying premiums. Universal Life policies often have this feature. Find out what the maximum amount you can borrow is and what would happen if you cancelled after borrowing. See if you can convert your policy to Term Life (though compare rates). See if you can convert your policy to what are called "Paid Up Adds" – this is insurance that is completely paid for. Figure out what the best option is for you using your Spend Smart skills.

HEALTH INSURANCE

- Look at the benefits of raising your deductible, even if your employer pays part of the premium.

- Many have HMO/Managed Care coverage - research your coverage and see if there are ways you can save money - even if the employer pays for health care many employees pay an increasing portion.

GENERAL

- Don't overlook disability coverage - need 60 to 75 percent of salary coverage until insured can return to work - eligibility period is key to controlling rate (1 month, 3 month, 6 month, etc.).

- Consider linking your car and home insurance. Some insurers will give you a better price (about 5% to 15% off) if you buy both policies from them. Having your home and auto policies with the same company may also be a requirement if you want to buy an "umbrella" policy, which extends your total liability coverage to, for example, $1 million. An umbrella policy is a worthy idea if you have a lot of assets to protect.

- Call for your state's insurance guide. More than half the states publish consumer guides with comparison prices and other useful data on the insurers that do business there. The information may not be totally up to date or a perfect match for your situation, but it's a good place to start. Phone your state insurance department for details. MN: 612-296-6848.

- Shop both independent and "captive" agents. Independents represent a number of companies and can, in theory at least, get you competitive price quotes. (Note, though: The rap on independents is that some of them may be cozy with just one or two high-priced companies.) Captive, or "exclusive" agents, represent a single company -- often a big one such as Allstate or State Farm. Call as many agents as you have the time and patience to deal with, but try to get three price quotes at a minimum. You're likely to find quotes at least a hundred dollars apart for the very same coverage.

- Don't ignore the "direct writers." Who don't have agents. A handful of companies, including some very good ones, don't use agents at all, but instead sell directly to certain groups. Highly regarded USAA (800-531-8000), for example, sells its policies directly to active or reservist military officers and their families. GEICO sells directly to government employees.

CHAPTER SIXTEEN
LAWN SERVICE

- Logic of lawns - we spend money fertilizing and watering them - just for the privilege of cutting them more often.

- Cut your lawn short (about 2 inches) in spring so sunlight can reach the soil - thereafter cut at about 3 ½ inches - longer grass helps the soil retain moisture longer.

- Don't apply fertilizer as thick as manufacturer recommends - there are more nutrients then the lawn can take at once - save money - use a 1/3 dose now and 1/3 dose several weeks later. **Save $50 to $70 per year.**

- Lawns need about 1 inch of water per week - you use less water and time by giving the yard one good soaking a week rather than several sprinkles.

- Water in early morning or evening - watering at midday or on windy days can use three or four times as much water. Morning is better so the grass can dry out - avoid fungus.

- Americans over-water by nearly 30% - how long does it take to accumulate the recommended 1-inch of water? Do a one-time test - set up four cans at different distances from the sprinkler and let the water run - check the cans every few minutes and note the time it takes each can to get an inch of water - add up the four times and divide by four - this is the amount of time you should water once per week. Of course, the amount of time you will water depends on the amount of rain you have had in the last week.

- Sharp lawnmower blades reduce the need for pesticides and weed control - get your blade sharpened two or three times a season.

- The number one cause of mower breakdowns? - corrosion, eating away at the body - spend a minute after each mowing cleaning it - spray the bottom off with a hose - wipe the top down with a wet rag - Armor All protects the bottom of your mower keeps grass from sticking and inhibits rust.

- Run the mower until it runs out of gas at the end of the season - start with fresh gas each season - otherwise you can gum up your carburetor.

CHAPTER SEVENTEEN
MEDICAL

- Colds and Flu run their cycle and go away on their own - there is nothing a doctor can prescribe or do that will limit the amount of time you are sick - save your money on doctor's visits for these items.

- Penicillin or other antibiotics will not speed your recovery from cold or flu - these illnesses are caused by viruses - antibiotics are for bacterial infections - NOT THE SAME!

- Doctors often prescribe what patients want - even antibiotics for cold and flu - because they know a patient who expects a remedy will be disappointed if they leave empty-handed - plus there is always the potential for a placebo effect. Unfortunately, this can cause you to purchase medication that may have no benefit (though the doctor wouldn't prescribe anything that would cause harm) - why buy medicine that won't help - always ask the doctor - "if you had these symptoms, what would you prescribe for yourself?"

- Don't buy the "all-in-one" cold medicines that handle every possible symptom - buy single ingredient medications (specifically the store-brands) to ease specific symptoms. You don't have symptoms all at once - if you have a cough, don't take a medicine for coughs and colds - you'll pay more for that medicine than just a cough suppressant.

Medications for specific symptoms

- muscle aches, fevers, headaches and pain - use aspirin, acetaminophen or ibuprofen.

- sore throats - use lozenges or sprays with phenol compounds, benzocaine, hexylresorcinol or menthol.

- coughs - use dextromethorphan for cough suppression- guaifenesin for expectorant.

- congestion - use psuedoephedrine or diphenhydramine.

- Compare ingredients (especially active ingredients - the drugs) on the name brand you usually buy to the store brand - the store brands usually have the exact same ingredients in the exact same dosages - often, the store brand is displayed right next to the name brand - save a minimum of $1 to $3 per bottle - **Save $10 to $30 per year.**

- Extra-strength pain relievers are extra expensive - the only difference is the number of milligrams of pain reliever per pill and the price per milligram - don't buy them - if you need extra strength take three regular pills (3 times 325 mg each = 975 mg) instead of two extra strength (2 times 500 mg each = 1000 mg). Maximum adult dosages for aspirin and acetaminophen are 1000 mg every four hours - maximum ibuprofen dose is 800 mg every eight hours - in terms of pain relief, 200 mg ibuprofen equals about 600 mg acetaminophen or aspirin.

- Chewable tablets cost 2 times the liquid equivalent

- Hospital billing errors are quite common - review your bill completely as soon as possible, especially if you pay a portion of it - average size of error is $1250!

- The APA (American Psychological Association) has studied subliminal tapes and found consistently they do not help lose weight, stop smoking, etc. 2 out of 3 people believe such programs work and spend 60 million per year on these.

CHAPTER EIGHTEEN
MISCELLANEOUS

BATTERIES

There are 3 types of batteries - use general purpose for seldom-used devices - alkaline for frequently used devices.

- Inexpensive General Purpose - 41 cents/hour

- Heavy Duty - 31 cents/hour

- Alkaline - 15 cents/hour

- Alkaline cost 3 to 4 times as much as regular batteries, but they last 9 to 10 times longer.

- No difference between brands in terms of battery life - buy what's on sale.

- Alkaline have 3 to 4-year shelf life - others have 9-month shelf life.

- Rechargeable NiCad batteries pay for themselves in several months if used often. If you use 20 or more AA or AAA batteries a year you'll come out ahead.

- Minimize battery use with AC adapter.

COMPLAINTS

- If things aren't right - TELL SOMEONE. Today, many companies recognize the value of keeping customers happy and will pay (perhaps refund or additional merchandise) to help turn dissatisfied customers into satisfied customers - first contact the store at the local level where the problem occurred or came from - start with the clerk, move to a manager if not satisfied - most problems will be resolved.

- If you are willing to take the time, go directly to the president of the company - write a letter listing the facts and explain what you want - be nice and non-threatening - emphasize how disappointed you are but that you are confident you will be taken care because you know the company is respectable. I remember my father once called the president of a shoe company when my brother's new tennis shoes wore out in a few weeks - end result? My three brothers and I each got a new pair of shoes!

DENTAL

- The TV commercials show people putting toothpaste the full length of the brush and halfway back again - guess what - 1/3 the length of the brush will suffice! Most people put toothpaste the full length of the brush and most of the paste gets spit out! If you use a tube of toothpaste a month, you can **save $20 per year.**

- After eating, if you can't brush, rinse your mouth with water - it's easy and free and washes out a substantial amount of bacteria and food particles.

- You get the same benefit from mouthwash by using a third of the recommended amount.

MAIL ORDER

- You can save 25 to 50% off local retail - also save sales tax if the firm is out of state - you may pay shipping however.

- Do your research, models, options, etc. before you buy - get several quotes.

- Ask about money-back guarantees - pay with a credit card so you can decline payment if you are not satisfied.

- Don't pay shipping insurance - legally, it is the shipper's responsibility to see the shipment gets to you undamaged.
- Don't waste money on lottery tickets - with 1 in 10 million odds of winning the grand prize (considered good odds) - even if you bought 10 one dollar tickets every week for 9,600 YEARS your odds of NOT WINNING are still better than your odds of Winning! Of course if you invested that money instead for 30 years, you would have $97,176 dollars on your investment of $10/week (total investment $15,600).

- In general, August and January are best months for retail sales as stores are making the transition from one season to another.

CHAPTER NINETEEN
Resale Means Spend Smart Savings For You

What do we do when we need garden tools, or skates for the kids or a dresser for the guest bedroom? We go to the store and buy it, right? Of course, since we are students of Spend Smart, we are going to shop around, watch for sales, and pay cash for the item so that we can save as much money as possible. What if we told you however, there is a way to save as much as 90% or more on many purchases we make?

You can do this, but it requires a change in our thinking. As discussed in the chapter on the Psychology of Buying, we need to re-think our habits. If you are willing to rethink a basic premise of how we buy, you have the opportunity to discover a huge Spend Smart Strategy which will easily put hundreds of dollars in your pocket every year. This strategy can be stated as:

WHY BUY NEW WHEN SLIGHTLY USED WILL DO?

When we need to buy something, most of us don't even consider the idea of buying it used (except perhaps a car). For various reasons, there are some products that you have to buy new. Consumable items like shampoo or toothpaste for example or one time use items like paint or lawn fertilizer. There are other items that you probably wouldn't want to buy used like some types of clothing (underwear!) or a fire extinguisher.

When you think about it however, there are probably dozens of purchases you make each year where perhaps a used item could meet your need and save you big bucks. For example, our oldest daughter has a nice matching bedroom furniture set purchased used for $100. My son wears a quality pair of hockey skates that cost $5. I enjoy riding my $10 ten-speed bike with the kids.

CHANGE YOUR THINKING AND SAVE HUNDREDS IF NOT THOUSANDS OF DOLLARS A YEAR BUYING USED!

Some people have a problem with buying used items. It usually has to do with one's ego. How can I buy something used? What if my friends see me? What will the neighbors think? I too had a problem with buying used items before I became a student of Spend Smart, before I realized the true value of a dollar. Not only would I buy everything new, I would typically buy the higher priced products!

Once I put my ego aside however and rationally considered the subject of buying used goods, I realized what buying used products could do to my financial picture. Perhaps the idea of buying used items instead of new doesn't immediately appeal to you. Remember, with Spend Smart you are in control of your financial destiny. You need to feel comfortable with whatever you choose to do with Spend Smart.

One key to feeling comfortable, to changing the way you think is to change our description of used items. The word "used" can bring up negative images in people's minds. Let's start using a different term as we begin to change our think about this subject. The term "Resale" is becoming a popular replacement term for "used".

Even if you think buying Resale items would magically turn you into a hobo, open your mind for a moment and at least consider the possibilities. Most people are able to buy some Resale items without damaging their dignity. Some types of items obviously make more sense to buy on a resale basis than others. Lets look at some general categories where resale items make the most sense for many people.

In general, there are several Spend Smart rules to apply in determining whether it makes sense to buy certain items used. These are summarized in the table below:

Spend Smart Resale Rules	
Buy Resale If...	Why?
• You don't use it very often	Durability isn't as important
• It has a long life span	It won't wear out soon
• It's for your kids	They will outgrow it soon
• It depreciates quickly	If it wears out you can buy another

Let's look at these rules more closely to determine what products might make sense to buy on a resale basis.

Many products are things we only use occasionally or at certain times of the year. In this case, the item has a large number of uses left. Products like lawn & garden equipment, sporting goods and books can fall into this category (you usually only read a book once right?)

Certain types of products are rugged and last a long time. Even if you use them often they don't wear out quickly. Products like hand tools, some types of furniture and compact discs last along time.

We buy many things for our children. Though kids can be tough on anything, they also outgrow some things before the wear them out. Products like coats, shoes and bicycles are good examples.

Some items depreciate quickly, even though they have years of useful life left. You probably can buy two of these items on a resale basis for less than the cost of a new one and get more use out of them. These can include large ticket items like cars, boats and recreational vehicles.

While you can save a lot of money buying used, or resale products, there are some types of products where it might not make sense to do so. Appliances are a good example. Newer appliances tend to be more energy efficient than older ones. Though you may save money on the purchase, those savings can be eaten up with energy costs. Therefore, you need to consider maintenance and energy costs when considering the purchase of some resale items.

SPEND SMART RULES EXCEPTION – RESALE COMPUTERS CAN ACTUALLY COST MORE THAN NEW PRODUCTS!

Computers and computer equipment can be the rare type of product where prices continue to go down over time as technology advances. The common cliché of course is that a computer is outdated as soon as you buy it. Today you can often buy a new computer for less than a previously owned computer.

Typically, the only way you save money buying a resale computer is if you buy a previous generation (e.g. Pentium instead of Pentium II processor) unit. This may be fine however if your needs don't call for the latest technology. This is also true with electronic equipment like TVs. For example, you probably can buy a nice 29-inch color TV for $300. If you don't care about the size of the TV however, you might be able to buy a 19-inch TV resale for $100.

Don't let these rare exceptions prevent you from considering buying resale products however. Resale can save you hundreds (or maybe even thousands if you have kids) of dollars every year. These are real Spend Smart dollars that you can put in your pocket. Of course, if you want to save money by buying resale, you need to know where you can find good condition resale items.

Oh Where Oh Where have those Resale Bargains Gone?

In most cases, you won't find resale products at the same places where you buy new products. Why would the retailer want to make less money by selling resale items? You might be surprised to learn that resale items are actually a growing segment of the retail market. Let's look at places to find resale items.

Resale Stores

Much more than the consignment stores of the past, specialty resale stores are booming. There are a number of chains which specializes in specific types of resale products. Many of these stores also buy items from individuals so if you have things you're not using, you have an easy way to "cash them in". Of course, just like when selling a car, if you take the time to sell them yourself, you'll probably make more money. Here's a few stores that have a growing number of locations across the nation:

Once Upon a Child®

With over 200 stores nationwide, Once Upon a Child is the largest chain of children's resale stores. They buy and sell new and "gently-used" children's toys, furniture and clothing. Think of how much you spend on children's items and check out the store nearest you. You can find the nearest store by visiting www.ouac.com on the Internet.

Play it Again Sports®

Play it Again Sports is probably the largest resale chain of any type with over 675 stores in North America. With the continuing fitness craze in the US, they always have a good variety of exercise and sports items. Access www.playitagainsports.com on the Web for the site nearest you.

Half Price Books

A fairly new company in the resale market, Half Price Books offers book at, you guessed it, HALF PRICE compared to new. They have a huge selection of books as well as videotapes and software. Currently, they operate in 10 states with 60 stores. Go to www.halfpricebooks.com to find the location nearest you.

Computer Renaissance®

Computer Renaissance was one of the first resale chains to appear with over 250 stores nationwide. Though used computers are not always a good value, they sell new systems to so you have a side-by-side opportunity to decide what the best value is for you. Check out www.cr1.com on the Web to find locations.

Retool®

Though they only began opening stores in 1998, Retool seems like a great option for buying hand and power tools. Go to www.re-tool.com for more information.

All these stores offer previously owned items in very good condition. They also give you the opportunity to turn your old items into cash! Though you could probably sell items for more at your own garage sales or through a classified ad, if you don't want to invest the time to do that, turn your "trash" into cash!

There are other types of stores you should visit to become familiar with the resale merchandise they offer. That way, if you need something they have in the future, you won't automatically spend extra money buying a new item. These include:

Pawn Shops

Pawn shops have a seedy reputation from the past, but a number of national chain pawn shops have made a conscious effort to appeal to typical consumers by offering a wide variety of merchandise such as home electronics, jewelry, musical instruments and much more.

Goodwill Industries

Goodwill welcomes all customers because it helps fund their charitable works. Merchandise is donated to Goodwill. Anything that doesn't sell in a reasonable time is then donated to the needy. So anything they sell helps fund their mission. You find clothing and household good here typically. Swallow your pride and put more money in your pocket by checking out Goodwill.

Not all good resale merchandise is found in traditional stores. Some of the best bargains you will ever see are found when you purchase directly from the current owner. It can take a little more effort to find what you are looking for, but it may be worth your time. Direct purchases can be found by looking through:

Garage Sales

If you think all you can get at garage sales is junk, think again. If you want to find excellent quality items at garage sales, the best way to do it is to go to garage sales in the better neighborhoods. Of course, when you go to a garage sale, you want to go there early for the best items. If you wait until the last day of the sale however, you can usually bargain down the prices. I had wanted some new golf clubs, but didn't want to spend hundreds of dollars. I recently stopped at a garage sale and bought 2 Taylor-Made metal woods that retail for $199 each for $10 each. One caution about garage sales however – they can lead to impulse buying so be careful or you'll be having a garage sale soon yourself!

Classified Ads

Classified ads can be a less-time consuming way to find resale items you are looking for because they organized by category. There are even specialty newspapers, such as PennySaver, that are devoted to classified advertising.

Summary

Next time you need to purchase something other than consumable items (food, gas, etc.) consider purchasing a resale product. Become familiar with the resale stores in your area and the merchandise they carry. That way when you need something, you will already have an idea whether you can purchase a good resale item.

Decide for yourself whether it is more important to you to achieve your Spend Smart goals or to protect your ego by buying everything new. Begin checking out the classified ads for things that you know you might purchase in the future so you can become familiar with what is available at what price. Go to some garage sales in nice neighborhoods to become familiar with what is sold.

You cannot make a good decision about what you would feel comfortable buying on a resale basis until you become educated. Even if you initially feel uncomfortable about buying resale items, as you become familiar with your options, you will find some items you are comfortable with. Spend Smart is about choices. We offer suggestions, but only you can decide what works for you.

Resale is one of the hidden goldmines in Spend Smart. Typically, you will find more items for sale on a resale basis then there are people who are buying them. Take advantage of this opportunity and you will significantly increase your Spend Smart success!

CHAPTER TWENTY
UTILITIES

Typical Americans spend $1000 to $2000 per year on energy usage. Obviously, this is one of the primary areas where you can utilize Spend Smart Strategies to save money without drastically changing your lifestyle.

Typical energy use (US Department of Energy):

Heating and Cooling – 46%
Lights and Appliances – 24%
Water Heating – 15%
Refrigeration – 15%

We've already looked at the costs of Water Heating, Appliances and Refrigeration in Chapter 7. Let's look at Heating/Cooling and Lights.

HEATING/COOLING

- Insulate your hot water heater with a water heater blanket – reduce heat loss and **save $35 per year.**

- Each degree warmer on your furnace raises your heating cost 3% - you can save 15% on heating by keeping the thermostat at 65 during the day and 60 at night instead of 70 and 65.

- Air conditioning is more expensive - each degree of cooling is a 5% increase in cost - set the thermostat at 77 instead of 70 means a 35% decrease in A/C costs.

- Replace your heating/cooling filters once per month.

- Close off unused rooms and shut the heating/cooling vents – for each room you shut the vents in - **save between $35 to $60 per year.**

- Turn down the heat or A/C when you are leaving the house - even if for a short time.
- Keep your house warmer - use ceiling fans to blow warm air down from the ceiling into the living area.

- Turn the heat down to 55 during the day if you will be gone.

- In winter, close drapes after the sun sets – for each window, snug-fitting drapes will save $6 per year.

- On sunny winter days, open the drapes to warm your house.

- Put aluminum foil behind radiators - this reflects heat into the room – for each radiator you have, reduced heating costs will **save $5 per year.**

- Reduce heat loss in the garage by tacking ¾ inch foam pipe insulation to the bottom of the garage door.

- After using the oven, turn off the oven and open the door to heat the kitchen.

- Save 15 percent or more from your summer electric bills – check into your electric company's program for installing a Energy Saver's Switch on your air conditioner - **save $75 per year.**

Annual Heating Cost Comparison (typical northern climate) from Northern States Power Company:

Electric Forced Air Furnace	$1,214
Propane Furnace	$874
Fuel Oil Furnace	$830
Electric Thermal Storage	$611
Standard Natural Gas Furnace	$541
High Efficiency Natural Gas	$421
Ground Source Electric Heat Pump	$389

Heating Cost Assumptions:

The following data were used to figure the annual heating costs listed on the previous chart:

- 1,500 square foot home (finished space).

- Electric Thermal Storage costs assume a limited off-peak service rate of 0.0264/kwh.

- Other electric heat rates assume standard electric space-heating rate of $0.0743/kwh June to September; $0.052/kwh other months.

- Standard furnaces are 80% efficient.

- High-efficiency furnaces are 90% efficient.

- Ground-source heat pump has a COP (efficiency rating) of 3.12; cost does not include cooling operation.

- Fuel costs: Propane = $0.76/gallon; Fuel oil = $0.95/gallon; Natural gas = $0.46/therm.

- Many energy companies offer rebates of $200 or more for installing qualifying high-efficiency gas furnaces or boilers. Natural gas furnaces with an efficiency of 92% or greater and boilers with an efficiency of 83% or greater are usually eligible for rebates. These are the same high-efficiency furnaces and boilers that can save you hundreds of dollars every year in heating costs.

- How to get a rebate? - When you buy your new high-efficiency natural gas furnace or boiler, ask your local heating contractor or dealer for the rebate form. Fill it out, send it in, and NSP will send you your rebate. It's that easy. (Allow six weeks for processing).

- A new high efficiency natural gas furnace or boiler will save money on your heating bill every month. High-efficiency equipment can cut your heating costs by as much as 35% because it burns less gas to generate the same amount of heat, saving you hundreds of dollars each year.

LIGHT BULBS

Believe it or not, big cost savings can be had with your light bulbs if you switch from typical incandescent bulbs to compact fluorescent bulbs. The two primary reasons for savings are the fact that fluorescent bulbs give off about 5 times as much light with the same wattage. That means a 20 watt fluorescent bulb gives off as much light as a 100 watt incandescent bulb. Source NSP (www.nspco.com).

Incandescent Bulbs

Wattage	Electric Cost/hour	Hours used each day	Electric Cost/day
150	1¢	2 - 7	60¢ - $2.10
100	<1¢	2 - 7	42¢ - $1.47
75	<1¢	2 - 7	43¢ - $1.10
60	<1¢	2 - 7	25¢ - 88¢

Compact Fluorescent

Wattage	Electric Cost/hour	Hours used each day	Electric Cost/day
30 (instead of 150)	<1¢	2 - 9	12¢ - 51¢
22 (instead of100)	<1¢	2 - 9	9¢ - 42¢
20 (instead of 75)	<1¢	2 - 9	8¢ - 38¢
15 (instead of 60)	<1¢	2 - 9	6¢ - 28¢

- Assuming average rates of 9 cents per kilowatt hour, a 100-watt bulb burns 9 cents of electricity in 10 hours of use - not much unless you've got dozens of bulbs on at the same time!

- Total of all light bulb usage multiplied by average length of use per day - maybe 800 watts times 3 hours per day = 2.4 kilowatt hours per day = $78.84 per year.

- Regular incandescent bulbs have changed little in the century since Edison invented them - 90% of electricity is wasted in heat - fluorescent bulbs are 3 to 4 times more efficient.

- Compact fluorescent bulbs cost $14 to $18 per bulb, so they are best used in lights that are often on - but they last 10 times longer and use ¼ of the electricity - they pay for themselves in a year or two and then you save $8 to $16 per year for the next 4 to 6 years.

- Many utility companies offer a rebate on fluorescent bulbs - cut your cost in half.

- Halogen bulbs for "flood lights" cost twice as much, but a 90 watt halogen ($10) puts out as much light as a standard 150 watt ($5) - power savings of 40% - halogen will last a little longer - you will save an average of $10 in electricity with the halogen light over the life of the bulb - the cost of the halogen bulb is replaced by the electricity savings.

- The odd watt bulbs (52, 67 and 90) are marketed as energy savers because of reduced electricity costs - however, they cost 50% and you get less light - is that a bargain?

- It is less expensive to light with fewer higher watt bulbs than more lower watt bulbs - One regular hundred watt bulb provides more light than two 60 watt - six 25 watt bulbs match the light of one 100 watt bulb.

- Christmas tree bulbs are cheap substitutes for night light bulbs.

- See the light on efficient lighting. Here's a stunning statistic: According to the Energy Department, fully 50% of the power Americans use for lighting is wasted, either because of inefficient equipment or plain old bad habits (like leaving the lights on in unoccupied rooms).

TELEPHONE

- If you make many calling card calls, bypass the standard calling cards offered by the Big Three. They're the ones with those hefty surcharges of 80¢ per call (79¢ with MCI). Instead, go for a card issued by an upstart like American Travel Network, which levies no surcharges whatsoever and charges a flat rate of 17.5¢ a minute.

- With most long-distance companies, including the Big Three, if you talk for two minutes and one second, your call gets rounded up to three minutes.

- Choose a service which doesn't round your calls off to the next full minute – you want to be billed in six-second increments - save as much as 20%.

- Watch out for in-state calls - If you make a lot of long-distance calls within your state, chances are they are being carried by your local phone company's network: In many cases, its prices won't be the best. However, it is possible to bypass the local phone company's regional long-distance services in 34 states using a long-distance carrier's access code. In some situations, punching these extra numbers -- or programming them into your phone's quick-dial feature -- can mean a large savings.

- Someone you know, or someone they know, can sign you up for 24 hr day long distance service at 10 cents/minute or less - find out who...then you don't have to worry about time of day calling...

WATER COSTS

- Don't leave the water running while brushing your teeth - American Waterworks Association says the average person uses 10 gallons of water doing this - average household can save 30,000 gallons a year by doing this. **Save $75 per year.**

- Don't run hot water while shaving? 7,000 gallons/year plus hot water costs - **Save $70 per year.**

HOW TO SAVE WATER - FROM AMERICAN WATERWORKS ASSOCIATION:

Activity	Normal Use	Conservative Use
Shower	Water Running 25 Gallons	Get wet, turn water off to soap up, then rinse - 4 Gallons
Tub Bath	Full Tub = 36 gallons	Minimal water = 10 to 12 gallons
Dishwashing	Tap running - 30 gallons	Fill sink with water - 5 gallons
Automatic Dishwasher	Full Cycle - 16 gallons	Short Cycle - 7 gallons
Washing hands	Tap running - 2 gallons	Fill wash basin - 1 gallon

- Putting a filled 2 liter bottle in your toilet bowl saves about 2000 gallons of water per year - **save $5 per person per year.**

- Leaking toilets (caused by a leaking flush valve) can waste 150 gallons of water per day without you knowing it - as much as 8 gallons per hour can leak in a bad scenario, costing $85 dollars per year in water and $100 per year in additional sewer charges - if you hear the toilet running to refill itself often there is a problem - check by putting a few drops of food coloring in the tank - check the bowl in 15 minutes to see if colored water has leaked through - flush valve replacement kits cost about $5.

- Fix leaky faucet - six drops per minute equals 1356 gallons per year!

- Keep a bottle of tap water for drinking in the refrigerator - avoid running water down the drain while waiting for it to get cold.

- Install a low flow shower head - saves 20 gallons every five minutes.

- If you will be gone more than 3 days, turn off your water heater if it is protected from freezing.

Appendix A

Best Time to Buy

Most items we buy are subject to seasonal price fluctuations. There are certain times of the year when the prices are lower than normal and there are other times when the prices are higher than normal. For example, air conditioner prices are lowest in January and highest in July.

Why are prices higher at some times and lower at others? Prices fluctuate and change because product demand and product supply change. The Law of Supply and Demand explains changing prices.

Economics tell us that supply and demand determine price. When more people want something, the demand increases and prices go up. When less people want something, the demand decreases and prices go down. When there is a product shortage, when supplies of a product are low, prices go up. When there is a product surplus when supplies of a product are high, prices do down.

Here's a summary of supply and demand that doesn't require a degree in economics to understand:

		DEMAND DECREASE	PRICES DOWN	DEMAND INCREASE	PRICES UP
SUPPLY DECREASE	PRICES UP	**NO CHANGE**		**PRICE INCREASE**	
SUPPLY INCREASE	PRICES DOWN	**PRICE DECREASE**		**NO CHANGE**	

If Supply and Demand change in the same direction, then they have an opposite effect on price, the cancel each other out. When Supply and Demand change in the opposite directions, they have the same effect on price and increase the effect.

Let's put this into plain English. The best time to buy a product is when other people aren't very interested in it (demand is low) but the stores have an overstock (supply is high). The worst time to buy a product is when everyone wants one (Demand is high) and most stores are sold-out (Supply is low).

Every year some toy becomes the "hot" Christmas toy of the year. In 1998, the hot product was the Furby. You could tell demand was high because people would line up for hours waiting for stores with Furbies to open. Supply was low because most stores were sold out. With the high Demand and low Supply, Furby prices were sky high.

Every spring, most ski equipment stores have huge sales. Since the skiing season is almost over, most people aren't thinking about buying equipment, and demand is low. The stores want to sell all "old" equipment so they will have room in the fall for the new equipment so the supply of old equipment is high. With low demand and high supply, prices are decreased in order to increase demand and get rid of the supply.

When more people want something, the demand increases and prices go up. When less people want something, the demand decreases and prices go down. When there is a shortage of a product, if the supply goes down, prices go up. When the supply of a product is low, when a product is hard to find, prices go up. This is the Law of Supply and Demand.

What does this mean in terms of Spend Smart? Every year, manufacturers come out with new or improved products. When manufacturers have a new product, they first try to sell their entire supply of the old product, because they won't sell much once the new one becomes available.

So typically, the best time to buy many products is right before the new or improved products come out. When the demand is low for the old product and the supply is much more than a store wants, they will keep lowering prices until all the old product is sold. For example – summer products are at their lowest price at the end of the summer – winter products are at their lowest price at the end of the winter.

The following list shows the best months to get the lowest prices on different products:

MONTH	ITEMS
JANUARY	Air Conditioners, Appliances, Baby Carriages, Bicycles, Books, Briefcases, Carpets & Rugs, China & Glassware, Christmas Items (Wrap, ornaments, etc.), Clothing - Athletic wear, Clothing - Children Winter Coats Clothing - Men's Overcoats, Clothing - Men's Shirts, Furniture, Hand Tools, Meats (Turkey/Ham), Pocketbooks, Shoes – Athletic, Toys, White Goods (Sheets, Towels, etc.)
FEBRUARY	China & Glassware, Clothing – Men's, Furniture, Lawn and Garden Supplies, Radios, Shoes – Women's, Sportswear & Equipment, Stereos, Storm Windows, Toys, TVs
MARCH	Clothing – Infant, Frozen Foods, Garden Supplies, Home health-care equipment, Ice Skates, Luggage, Shoes – Kids, Ski Equipment, TVs, Washing Machines
APRIL	Flooring, Hosiery, Linens, Paint, Tools
MAY	Auto Accessories, Jewelry, Ketchup, Mustard, Outdoor Furniture, Power Tools, Tires, TVs
JUNE	Beer, Clothing - Men's, Floor Coverings, Juice, Ketchup, Mustard, Shoes – Men's, Shoes - Women's
JULY	Bathing Suits, Beer, Briefcases, Clothing – Children, Clothing - Men's Shirts, Clothing – Summer, Furniture, Juice, Shoes - Men's, Shoes – Women's
AUGUST	Air Conditioners, Bathing Suits, Beer, Carpeting, Cosmetics, Furniture, Grills, Juice, Soda, Tires, White Goods (Sheets, Towels, etc.)
SEPTEMBER	Bicycles, Car Batteries, Car Mufflers, Garden Equipment, Hardware, Paint
OCTOBER	Appliances, Bicycles, Ceiling Fans, Clothing - Fall/Winter, Clothing – Jeans, Fishing Equipment, Golf Equipment, Home Health-Care Equipment, Linens, Shoes - Men's
NOVEMBER	Appliances, Blankets & Quilts, Clothing – Jeans, Clothing - Men's Suits & Coats, Clothing – Winter, Home Improvement Supplies, Real Estate – Homes, Water Heaters
DECEMBER	Baby Furniture, Blankets & Quilts, Clothing – Children, Coats & Hats, Power tools

Here is the same information in: Alphabetical Order by Product (Page 1):

ITEM	MONTH
Air Conditioners	August
Air Conditioners	January
Appliances	January
Appliances	November
Appliances	October
Baby Carriages	January
Baby Furniture	December
Bathing Suits	August
Bathing Suits	July
Bicycles	January
Bicycles	October
Bicycles	September
Blankets & Quilts	December
Blankets & Quilts	November
Books	January
Briefcases	January
Briefcases	July
Car Batteries	September
Car Mufflers	September
Carpeting	August
Carpets & Rugs	January
Ceiling Fans	October
China & Glassware	February
China & Glassware	January
Christmas Items (Wrap, ornaments, etc.)	January

ITEM	MONTH
Clothing - Athletic wear	January
Clothing - Children	December
Clothing - Children	July
Clothing - Children Winter Coats	January
Clothing - Fall/Winter	October
Clothing - Infant	March
Clothing - Jeans	November
Clothing - Jeans	October
Clothing - Men's	June
Clothing - Men's Overcoats	January
Clothing - Men's Shirts	January
Clothing - Men's Shirts	July
Clothing - Men's Suits & Coats	November
Clothing - Summer	July
Clothing - Winter	November
Coats & Hats	December
Cosmetics	August
Fishing Equipment	October
Floor Coverings	June
Flooring	April
Frozen Foods	March
Furniture	February
Furniture	January
Furniture	July
Furniture	August

ITEM	MONTH
Garden Equipment	September
Garden Supplies	March
Golf Equipment	October
Grills	August
Hand Tools	January
Hardware	September
Home health-care equipment	March
Home health-care equipment	October
Home Improvement Supplies	November
Hosiery	April
Houses	November
Ice Skates	March
Jewelry	May
Ketchup, Mustard	June
Ketchup, Mustard	May
Lawn and garden	February
Linens	April
Linens	October
Luggage	March
Meats (Turkey/Ham)	January
Men's Apparel	February
Outdoor Furniture	May
Paint	April
Paint	September
Pocketbooks	January
Power tools	December
Power tools	May

ITEM	MONTH
Radios, Stereos, TVs	February
Shoes - Athletic	January
Shoes - Kids	March
Shoes - Men's	July
Shoes - Men's	June
Shoes - Men's	October
Shoes - Women's	February
Shoes - Women's	July
Shoes - Women's	June
Ski Equipment	March
Soda, Beer, Juice	August
Soda, Beer, Juice	July
Soda, Beer, Juice	June
Sportswear & Equipment	February
Storm Windows	February
Tires	August
Tires and Auto Accessories	May
Tools	April
Toys	February
Toys	January
TVs	March
TVs	May
Washing Machines	March
Water Heaters	November
White Goods (Sheets, Towels, etc.)	August
White Goods (Sheets, Towels, etc.)	January

Appendix B

Save on Groceries by Helping Others

How would you like to save a minimum of $168 on groceries per year by doing the things you probably already do to help your family, neighbors and friends? Its possible by working with SHARE.

SHARE (Self-Help and Resource Exchange) is a national network of non-profit organizations dedicated to:

- providing quality monthly food packages at a reduced cost.

- promoting volunteer service in our communities.

- building partnerships with community organizations.

SHARE is a non-profit community building organization, offering a nutritious food package ($28-30 value) for $14.00 (14.50 in some areas) to anyone who is willing to give two hours of volunteer time in their community. SHARE is not a government program, but is funded by grants, donations, and the price of the food package. The savings are generated by the bulk buying power of all its members.

By pooling thousands of dollars across the nation, SHARE purchases food at wholesale prices and passes the savings on to participants. Volunteers distribute the food through a network of hundreds of Registration Sites across 33 states in the country.

SHARE is unique because it includes everyone. There are no qualifications to participate in SHARE. People become involved with SHARE because they want to Spend Smart AND because they enjoy helping others. Food packages are typically offered once a month. To sign up for a package, simply contact the SHARE location nearest you (see the table below).

Some people are concerned that SHARE is a public assistance program and they might not be eligible or they don't want to take away from someone who really needs the service. Nothing could be further from the truth...

SHARE IS NOT A CHARITY – SHARE IS A MONEY-SAVING OPPORTUNITY FOR THOSE WILLING TO HELP OTHERS!

SHARE food package is not donated food. The $14 each participant pays is pooled with thousands of others, so buying power is increased as each item is purchased on the open market. In this way, SHARE does not compete with food pantries and other food programs that rely on donated goods. The more people who participate in SHARE the better our buying power. So, tell a friend!

Everyone is eligible for SHARE! When you go to a neighborhood registration site, you simply pay $14 ($14.50 in some areas) in cash, food stamps, or a money order at the beginning of the month. Then you complete the two hours of community service sometime during the month, and pick up your package of groceries on Distribution Day at the end of the month.

Want to increase your savings? You can purchase as many SHARE packages as you would like as long as you do two hours of community service and pay $14 for each package that you purchase. There also are specialty packages to give you extra saving on items your family eats every month such as all-meat or vegetarian packages.

The main mission of the SHARE program is to bring together the community through low cost food distribution. The reason the SHARE program works so well is not only because of the low cost food part, but because of the bonds that it creates between people in the community. Every SHARE participant must do his or her two hours of community service in order to receive a SHARE package.

BEST OF ALL, YOU CHOOSE YOUR VOLUNTEER WORK!

SHARE doesn't assign community service projects, though they can offer suggestions if you need one. SHARE participants choose for themselves what they would like to do for their community service. The SHARE definition of volunteer community service is "anything you do for anyone else that you don't get paid for."

If you're already volunteering somewhere, then you're already doing your part! If not, then do something you like! Volunteer at your child's school, your place of worship, hospitals, libraries, or simply help out at your neighborhood SHARE Host Site or our SHARE warehouse!

Some people are concerned about the type or quality of food they will receive. The food package varies according to items that are in season. Every time you purchase a SHARE package you will receive a newsletter with the next month's food package, so there is never any guessing!

Every SHARE package (although it is different every month), contains 6-8 pounds of frozen meat, 4-6 fresh vegetables, 2-3 fresh fruits, 2-3 staple items (i.e. potatoes, pasta, rice, etc.) and 2-3 packaged or processed items (i.e. pancake mix, fig bars, etc.) All of the food in the SHARE package is high quality and is never second-hand or donated. Here is an example of a recent food package:

BEEF SIRLOIN TIPS, POLISH SAUSAGE, CHICKEN DRUMS, COOKED CHICKEN (WHITE MEAT CUBED) , POLLOCK FILLETS, CORN ON THE COB, HUNT'S MUSHROOM PASTA SAUCE, PASTA, LINGUINE, WAFFLES, SWISS MISS CHOCOLATE PUDDING, POTATOES, ONIONS, CARROTS, APPLES

AT $14, THAT IS A SUPER SPEND SMART DEAL!

Take advantage of SHARE – help yourself to Spend Smart savings while helping others. For information, contact the SHARE office nearest you.

SHARE-Baltimore 808 Barkwood Court Linthicum, MD 21090 (410) 636-9615 FAX (410) 636-9629	SHARE-Central Florida 3854-B S. Orange Avenue, Suite B Orlando, FL 32806 800-726-7427 (407) 858-0300 FAX (407) 858-0333
SHARE of Central Illinois 1825 NE Adams Street Peoria, IL 61603 800-637-5508 (309) 637-0282/88 FAX (309) 637-0307	SHARE-Cincinnati 2059 Ross Avenue Norwood, OH 45212 (513) 458-3030 FAX (513) 458-3032
SHARE-Colorado 9360 Federal Blvd. Denver, CO 80221 (303) 428-0609 800-933-7427 Fax (303) 427-4440	SHARE-Connecticut 122 Park Avenue Hartford, CT 06108 (860) 280-3111 (860) 520-1049 FAX (860) 280-3190
Community SHARE 320 S. Avon Rockford, IL 61102 (815) 961-7287 FAX (815) 961-0036	Heartland-SHARE 215 SE Quincy Topeka, KS 66603 (913) 234-6208 FAX (913) 234-3608
SHARE-Heart of the Carolinas 406 Deep Creek Road Fayetteville, NC 28301 P.O. Box 2009 Fayetteville, NC 28302 (910) 485-6923 FAX (910) 483-69731	SHARE-Iowa 1102 S. 7th Street P.O. Box 328 Oskaloosa, IA 52577-0328 (515) 673-4000 FAX (515) 673-6042
SHARE-Mid-Atlantic 1115 Tabb Street Norfolk, VA 23504-3427 800-253-7842 (757) 627-6599 FAX (757) 627-6389	SHARE-Mid-Michigan 2701 S. Martin L. King Blvd. Lansing, MI 48910 (517) 482-8900 FAX (517) 482-891

SHARE-New England 146 Will Drive P.O. Box 63 Canton, MA 02021 (617) 828-5151 FAX (617) 828-7470	SHARE-New Jersey 436 Ferry Street P.O. Box 5427 Newark, NJ 07105-3909 (201) 344-2400 FAX (201) 344-3532
SHARE-New York 1601 Bronxdale Avenue Bronx, NY 10462 (718) 518-1513 FAX (718) 518-7458	SHARE-Northern California 4075 Lakeside Drive Richmond, CA 94806 800-499-2506 (510) 222-2506 FAX (510) 222-3007
SHARE-Northern Ohio 250 Opportunity Parkway Akron, OH 44307 (330) 253-8806 FAX (330) 253-8836	SHARE-Philadelphia 2901 W. Hunting Park Avenue Philadelphia, PA 19129 (215) 223-2220 FAX (215) 223-3073
PrarieLand SHARE 1222 Bunn Avenue Springfield, IL 62703-5343 (217) 529-2500 FAX (217) 529-7030	SHARE of S.E. Wisconsin 13111 W. Silver Spring Drive Butler, WI 53007 (414) 783-2500 FAX (414) 783-2515
SHARE-Southern California 3350 "E" Street San Diego, CA 92102 (619) 525-2200 FAX (619) 525-2213	SHARE-Tampa Bay 1405 E. Second Avenue Tampa, Fl 33605 (813) 248-3379 FAX (813) 248-1355
Tri-State SHARE 415 Eleventh Street P.O. Box 428 Ambridge, PA 15003-0428 (412) 266-0470 FAX (412) 266-4916	SHARE -Central/Northern Vermont 888-742-7363
SHARE - Hardwick/Craftbury, VT 802-586-9958	SHARE-Virginia 106-B S. Franklin Street P.O. Box 570 Christiansburg, VA 24073-0570 (540) 382-6186
SHARE-Washington D.C. Metro 5170 Lawrence Place Hyattsville, MD 20781 (301) 864-3115 FAX (301) 864-5370	World SHARE 6950 Friars Road San Diego, CA 92108 (619) 686-5818 FAX (619) 686-5815

In the Minnesota, Iowa, North Dakota, South Dakota, Wisconsin Region, there is another organization known as FARE For All, which operates, similar to SHARE. If you live in one of these regions, you can contact FARE at 1-800-582-4291.

Appendix C

Spend Smart Survey

Answer the questions below. Write your answers in the spaces provided on page 4 in the Spend Smart workbook. These questions will help you get a quick overview of how Spend Smart™ strategies can mean money in your pocket. "You" means your entire household.

Question
1. How many boxes of cereal do you eat per week?
2. How many loads of laundry are hot water loads per week?
3. How many times per week do you buy food/drinks/snacks when you get gas?
4. How many people brush their teeth in your house?
5. How many degrees above 68 do you set the furnace at during the winter?
6. How many lbs. of hamburger does your family eat per week?
7. How many children do you have under age 7?
8. How many people use the shower in your household?
9. How many lottery tickets do you buy per week?
10. How many gallons of milk do you buy per week?
11. How many degrees below 78 do you set the air conditioner at in the summer?
12. How many people leave the water running when washing their hands?
13. How many times per week do you eat out for lunch?
14. How many times per week do you use a vending machine?
15. Do you participate in the SHARE food co-op?
16. Do you check your tire pressure monthly?
17. Do you rinse dishes before loading the dishwasher?
18. Do you (men) run hot water when shaving?
19. Is your auto insurance deductible $250 or less?

Appendix D

Watch the Cash Register – Because its your Money!

Almost every product we purchase today has a Universal Product Code or UPC. You know, those long, skinny, computer-ish lines and number. These get scanned when you buy something and the price automatically rings up on the cash register and prints on your receipt.

Retailers say that scanner technology has several benefits. It speeds checkout time, decreases labor costs and improves sales and inventory records. Best of all, the scanners are always right!

Of course, people sometimes make errors or forget to do something. The only way a store's computer system knows the price for an item is when a human tells it what the price is. Price maintenance has become a huge data-processing function for retailers. Imagine a grocery store where they have tens of thousands of different items. In any given week, the price may be changed on several thousand items.

Scanning errors can result in overcharges and undercharges. Some studies show that, overall, overcharges are balanced by undercharges. Overcharges can cost the individual shopper money, especially if the shopper doesn't speak up when they occur. They also can be frustrating for time-conscious consumers, who may have to stand in line for a refund, or worse, return to the store.

SPEND SMART SCANNER STRATEGIES

Now after you've gone to all the trouble to maximize your Spend Smart savings, are you going to let a computer rob you of your money? Spend Smart Shoppers, those who are aware of prices, check scanner charges for expensive items or items they know are on sale. They have written down the price for items on their shopping list and keep their eye on the cash register display.

If you find you have been overcharged, immediately point the item out to the cashier. Ask what the store's scanning-error policy is. These policies can vary:

- Some stores simply credit the error.
- Some stores give you a discount.
- Some stores GIVE YOU THE MIS-PRICED ITEM FOR FREE!

Now here's the bad news for students of Spend Smart. The FTC study shows that overcharges are more likely when it comes to sale-priced items. Since Spend Smart shoppers probably buy more items on sale than typical shoppers, that means...

SPEND SMART SHOPPERS GET OVERCHARGED MORE OFTEN!

The Price Check II study shows that overall scanning accuracy is high, however, 1 in 28 "Sale" items are priced incorrectly. The pricing errors for sale and non-sale items were about equal in number; however, overcharges accounted for two-thirds of the pricing errors on sale items. In other words...

THERE ARE TWICE AS MANY OVERCHARGES AS UNDERCHARGES WHEN AN ITEM IS ON SALE!

Here's some more statistics from Price Check II:

- The Price Check II inspections, which were carried out in 1,033 retail stores by weights and measures officials in 36 states and the U.S. Virgin Islands, found:

- One of every 30 items checked (3.35 percent) was mispriced. Half of these errors were undercharges and half were overcharges. A total of 107,096 items were checked.

- Each undercharge averaged $5.28, and each overcharge averaged $3.20. Two years earlier, each undercharge averaged $2.96, and each overcharge averaged $3.02.

- For sale items, pricing errors were found in 1 of every 28 items checked. Almost two-thirds of the errors found were overcharges; the remainder were undercharges.

- For non-sale items, pricing errors were found in 1 of every 32 items checked. Slightly more than one-third of the errors found were overcharges; the remainder were undercharges.

- Some stores have achieved outstanding pricing accuracy. In 43 percent, or 720 of the 1,669 inspections, no price errors were found.

- Most stores have acceptable pricing accuracy. 71 percent of the inspections, or 1,188 out of 1,669, "passed;" that is, at least 98 percent of the items checked were correctly priced.

- Some stores have pricing accuracy problems. 29 percent of the inspections did not pass; that is, less than 98 percent of the items checked were correctly priced. In these inspections, an average of 91 percent of the items checked were correctly priced.

- Wide variations were found in pricing accuracy from chain to chain and store to store. Among the types of stores inspected, food stores as a group had the highest pricing accuracy, while hardware stores as a group had the lowest pricing accuracy.

- The Price Check II inspections were carried out by weights and measures officials in Alabama, Alaska, Arizona, Arkansas, California, Colorado, Connecticut, Delaware, Florida, Georgia, Hawaii, Iowa, Idaho, Indiana, Kansas, Kentucky, Louisiana, Maine, Maryland, Michigan, Minnesota, Missouri, Montana, North Carolina, New Hampshire, New Jersey, Nevada, Ohio, Oklahoma, Pennsylvania, South Carolina, Tennessee, U.S. Virgin Islands, Utah, Vermont, Washington and West Virginia.

- Inspectors found that pricing errors on sale items resulted from numerous problems, including incorrect shelf and item prices, incorrect sign prices, out-of-date signs and incorrect prices in the computer. For errors on non-sale items, incorrect shelf and item prices were largely responsible.

- Copies of the 1998 and 1996 "Price Check" studies, as well as consumer and business education materials, are available from the FTC's web site at http://www.ftc.gov and also from the FTC's Consumer Response Center, Room 130, 600 Pennsylvania Avenue, NW, Washington, D.C. 20580; 202-FTC-HELP(202-382-4357); TDD for the hearing impaired 202-326-2502.

Technology is a wonderful thing for shoppers. It makes it easier for retailers to respond quickly to changes in local demand and prices on products. Scanners make it possible for prices to change on a weekly or even daily basis. This type of price fluctuation is a great Spend Smart opportunity.

The challenge for Spend Smart students to take advantage of this opportunity is that they must be aware of prices. They need to know when something is at a very low price, especially food items, so you can maximize savings by stocking up. Use the Grocery Scorecard (found in your workbook) to help you do this.

At the same time, Spend Smart practitioners must pay close attention as your items are being scanned, to make sure the sale price is charged. Two-thirds of scanning errors on sales items are overcharges. The best way to make sure you don't get overcharged it to use a shopping list, and write the price for every item on the list. That way you have an easy reference for checking scanning accuracy.

Appendix E
HALF AS MUCH

You can cut your use of consumable products in half if you remember one basic premise - manufacturers recommend you use more of their product than necessary – WHY?

There are two reasons. Manufacturers want to make sure the product lives up to their marketing claims. They also want to increase sales!

- Laundry detergent - if you have soft water, try using half the detergent and see how it works - should be just as clean.

- Dishwasher detergent - experiment, but if soft water, half should be fine.

- Toothpaste - most people can use 1/3 of what they use - if froth comes out of your mouth while brushing, that's wasted toothpaste.

- Liquid hand soap - a full stroke of the bottle pump gives you three times more soap than needed.

- Shampoo - lather, rinse, repeat - lather in your hair is cleaning power that hasn't been used - save the time, shampoo and water.

The typical family uses over $300 worth of these products each year. Use Half as Much and **save $150 per year!**

DISCLAIMER

The Spend Smart course and materials are meant to help you save money on your spending so you can use the money for other purposes. Great amounts of research and effort have gone into compiling this information and ensuring its accuracy. While the authors utilize many of the principles and ideas set forth, please be advised there may be mistakes, both typographical and in content, so it is up to you, the student of these materials to treat this book as a source of ideas but not as unquestionable truth.

Equally important, the authors cannot anticipate every possible situation and condition where information from the Spend Smart course could be used and therefore cannot predict all possible outcomes of using this information. It is possible in some circumstances that specific tips would not be valid or would be false.

It is therefore, the responsibility of the student or reader of these materials to decide for themselves whether advice from this course is appropriate for the reader's use in general and specific circumstances. The reader must determine potential risk for any course of action and accept that risk on their own accord if he or she proceeds. It is also the student's complete responsibility to test and verify Spend Smart advice before using advice that could result in physical harm and/or financial loss.

The author and publisher shall have neither liability nor responsibility to any person, group, or entity with respect to any loss or damage caused, or alleged to be caused, directly or indirectly by information contained in this book.

If you are unwilling to accept complete responsibility for your use and application of any information contained in the Spend Smart course and materials and are unwilling to be bound by all of the above, please return all materials to your course instructor for a full refund.